Beautifully Broken

From Brokenness to Healing Series, Book 2

by Pastor Dr. Donna Fox

Copyright © 2020 Donna Fox. All rights reserved.

No part of this book may be reproduced or transmitted in any form or by any means, electronic or mechanical, including photo-copying or recording, or by an information-storage-and-retrieval system—except in the case of brief quotations embodied in critical articles or by a reviewer who may quote short passages in a review to be printed in a magazine or newspaper or published on-line without permission in writing from the author.

Editor: Anthony Ambrogio

Cover Design: SOS Graphic Designs

Publisher: G Publishing LLC

ISBN: 978-1-7359426-2-9

Library of Congress Control Number: 2020924202

Published and Printed in the United States of America

Beautifully Broken

Dedication

I would like to dedicate this book to my parents, Alvin and Joyce Vaughn. Thank you for your unconditional love, even in the worst of times.

Mama, I have had many occasions to look back and regret all the hurt and pain that I must have caused you. As a parent and grandparent, I truly understand the many heartbreaks and disappointments that you must have encountered. I often catch myself gently whispering, "Mama, I'm so sorry," and praying that you can hear me. I sometimes still call your name! It gives me satisfaction when I simply say "Mama." I'm sure it's more for my own peace of mind, but I believe you know how very much I love you.

Daddy, I was told that you felt I needed to be pushed because I have a way of not finishing things. And you were right. There have been so many things that I started and did not finish. However, I know you would be well pleased with me now.

I will finish this race God has placed before me. Not only will I finish it, but I will finish strong.

I Love You Both Dearly

Acknowledgements

First, I want to give God All the Glory! I can do nothing without You Lord. Thank You! So grateful that He knows my name!

To my wonderful, devoted husband, Cornell Fox; I am nothing without you. Your unwavering love and support have brought me through so many rough times—times that I never mentioned, times when I didn't know if or how I was going to make it, times when I felt defeated and needed to be encouraged—you were there; you were there to just push me through, saying, "Let's just get through today." I'm forever grateful and humbled that God loved me so much to put you in my life; I Love You and I Honor You as you walk alongside me in ministry. Thank You!

To my first-born, Terrell "Terry" Vaughn (my son-husband), my protector. Always encouraging with a voice of reason, even as a child. You have given and continue to give me a different perspective, inspiration, and strength. Thank You, for loving and respecting me through my mess (good, bad, and ugly).

And, even as God has called me into "servanthood," you are still there to support, encourage and protect. As I look at the husband, father and grandfather that you have become, I realize I must have done *something* right. I am so grateful to be able to call you "son," and I love you with every ounce of my being. Thank You for serving alongside of me. I am truly Blessed.

To my son in heaven, James "Jay" Kennedy Jr, I love you more than words can say. There is not a day goes by that I don't look at your picture or think about you. I didn't understand then why you were having children so rapidly at such an early age, but now that I look back, I am so grateful for the three gifts you left me. I see you in each one of them (especially your grandchild who looks just like you). I Love You, my son.

My darling daughter Tiffany: after having your brothers I waited almost 10 years to have you, and I'm so grateful that I did. The enemy tried to take you from me, but God said, "Not so!" I love the confidence and boldness that you possess. I look at you and wonder what my life would have been like, if I had had just a little bit of what you possess.

I can't live life through you, but I'm so glad that I got to see you develop into such an amazing woman; a gorgeous (model-ready) wife, mother and daughter. I thank you for all of your love and support. Thank you for always being there, no matter what! I'm very grateful for your love as you walk with me in fulfilling my God-given assignment in GodsPeace Ministry. Love You more than words can say.

To my grandchildren and great-grandchildren, Nana loves you to life!

To my Bonus Mother and Father, Albert and Yvonne Fox; thank You for accepting me with loving and opened arms. I am forever grateful for your Love and respect.

To my parents Alvin and Joyce Vaughn, Thank You for loving me unconditionally.

To my Spiritual Dad, Pastor Leon Glover, Thank You for walking with me even when I didn't believe in myself. You were always there to encourage and motivate me to press on.

Although my parents and spiritual dad have gone home to be with the Lord, I know that they would be so proud.

To *Everyone* who have supported and continue to support me in ministry, I appreciate you all so very much. Thank You. I could not have done it without you.

Forward

Beautifully Broken: "From Brokenness to Healing"

Beautifully Broken is the second of a three-book series. It is a journey through my life with its many ups, downs and turns. There have been times when I have had to go forward and other times when I have had to retreat. This is a very personal journey to inner healing.

I have come to understand that, in order to become totally healed you may have to go back to those "hidden places" or secrets. Those are the places or events in our lives that we don't want to revisit, because of the pain, frustration, and even disappointment there. However, unless we uncover the source of our pain, we never really understand the true impact that such pain has had on our lives.

Through these writings, I have discovered so many things about myself. As a result of revisiting various points in my past, emotions that I thought I had overcome have resurfaced.

The Brokenness to Healing Series has taken me on a journey to inner healing, starting with *The Forgotten Child* and continuing here in *Beautifully Broken*.

This inner healing holds the key to many emotional and physical issues that I have had to experience throughout my life. The loneliness, rejection and even bitterness that operated in my life were a direct result of so many wrong choices. I have other things that I have yet to share, and I know that before this series is over my life will literally be an open book. It is my truth!

It is not my intention to offend anyone. However, in order for true repentance and forgiveness to take place, it requires total honesty from within. I pray that this series will help others face some of the pain of their past, knowing that only our faith in God will help us to prevail.

There is a lot that I have shared and much more that I have not. However, I depend on the Holy Spirit to lead and guide me as to what and when to release many of my experiences.

So, be patient with me, as I go through my own personal deliverance experience in an effort to help myself and others.

Table of Contents

Acknowledgements i
Forward v
1. New Beginnings 1
2. A Time of Peace 16
3. Rebounding 23
4. The Pregnancy 35
5. Relocating 44
6. He's Back 54
7. New Life, New Problems 61
8. Mister Fox 68
9. A Changed Life 77
10. Taking the Next Step 90
11. Saving My Mother's Honor 99
Beautifully Broken: To My Readers 120
Beautifully Broken: I Say a Little Prayer for You
.... 123

1. New Beginnings

July 27, 1977, this date will forever be etched in my mind. First of all, it is the day my older brother Bobby was sentenced to life in prison.

As we left the courtroom, everyone was down and heartbroken, especially my mother. I can only imagine how she must have felt, knowing that she would never be able to see her son free. He would never be able to come to dinner; he would never be able to spend time with her (unconditionally); he would never be able to come back home again. Although, we all knew we were coming to hear the sentencing pronounced over his life (life in prison without the possibility of parole), it still cut like a knife to hear those words.

As his sister, my pain was great, so to think of what feelings my mother was experiencing is heart wrenching. It was another blow to her mother/son relationship. He had been gone for so long in Japan, and now she was losing him again. The pain must have been unbearable. I'm sure she was dealing with the kind of grief you feel when someone dies— to be able to see your child but not be able to live life with him. It was almost as if he wasn't there at all.

Beautifully Broken

As we made our way home, everyone was quiet! The ride from downtown Detroit seemed to take an eternity. When we got home, everyone was just trying to come to grips with what had just happened. We were all looking around, trying to find some type of comfort in each other's eyes or looking for some hint of life, but there was nothing there. Only sadness!

Previously, at the urging of my mother I had accepted a marriage proposal from someone that I really didn't know.

First, I did not know if I was really in love with him or not. I know I was in Lust but wasn't quite sure if it was Love, real Love. My heart had recently been broken, and there was a part of me that was still hurting (even though I could not let anyone else know what I was truly feeling). Remember, I'm the "Forgotten Child," the one who knew how to keep secrets really well.

James and I enjoyed each other, we laughed and had fun, but I didn't love him the way I should have. My heart still belonged to someone else, and I didn't quite know how to handle it.

Looking back, I'm sure it was more lust than love. I think I knew it even then, because part of me wanted to get revenge on D. Smith for breaking my heart and leaving me with a baby, while he continued to parade girls in my face. Oh, how I hated that man! So, when I accepted the marriage proposal, it was out of anger and out of a desire to not disappoint my mother. Marriage is a lifelong commitment, and I knew it, but I accepted to please someone else.

I had been raised as someone always being overlooked; I knew my opinion really didn't matter. I had tried to say no, but it was met with disappointment from both James and my mother, so I gave in. Somehow, I do believe that as time went on, I "learned" to love him as much as I would allow myself to love him. I didn't really want to give all of me again. The last relationship left me battered, bruised, embarrassed, and ashamed. The nagging question, "What is wrong with me?" kept resurfacing. What was it about me that caused the man I really loved not to love me back?

The truth of the matter is I settled; I settled for someone that I thought loved me.

Beautifully Broken

Because, the man I really loved didn't love me the same way I loved him. It's a dangerous thing not to know your own self-worth!

James and I had already gone downtown and gotten our marriage license, but no date had been set. I think I was trying to prolong the engagement as long as possible.

When we were all sitting around the house after the sentencing, I'm not sure how the conversation came around to marriage, but someone suggested that James and I should get married! Right then, that very day! I was reluctant, but was anxious to change the mood of the house and replace the sadness on my mother's face with some type of joy (even if it cost me something that I really didn't want to do), so I said, "Yes, let's do it."

My fiancé's mother lived next door to us, and they had a minister in the family. Before I knew it, I was dressed and headed to my "shotgun wedding."

After we recited the vows, I felt no emotion; it really meant nothing. I was just going through the motions, trying to make everyone else happy. As we were coming home my oldest brother was blowing his car horn (as was the custom back then), and I was so embarrassed because I didn't want anyone to know. I wasn't ready to let the world know what a foolish decision I had made. I believe my husband was genuinely happy, though (or so it seemed).

We had a one-night honeymoon at a hotel on Jefferson while Mama kept my oldest son. Our honeymoon consisted of walking down to the Renaissance Center and walking back to the hotel, trying to be happy or at least giving the appearance of happiness.

We lived with my mother for a short while, and then we moved into our own apartment. That was a disaster. One of my father's sisters was still babysitting for mama. She invented a lot of lies and began to spread them through the family; it was so hurtful—not just to me but to my mother as well. I had gotten used to walking in a place of numbness, but why did they have to keep hurting and betraying mama? What did she ever do to them? She was always there whenever they called. Before surgeries, she was there. When bills needed to be paid, she was there. What was it? I've had so many lessons in learning how hard it can be to love your family. Yet, through it all, I still did.

I loved them all! I just wanted a relationship with them like the relationship they had with my sister Ella. But it never happened! I still love them though!

After all that, Mama was right there. She helped us find and furnish the apartment. Then she came to visit every day. I mean EVERY DAY! I believe she was living her life through us, trying to get something that she wanted or missed (since my father had passed). As I look back, my heart goes out to her, because I know her pain had to be great. But she never complained or showed it. (Remember, we kept our real feelings inside—secrets). Never did we discuss how I felt or even how she felt. Life goes on, or so we thought.

Eventually, my mother would purchase a home on the west side of Detroit, and we moved in. It was a two-family flat so she would be able to keep her family close. At the time she purchased the house, I didn't know if she planned on moving into the downstairs flat or if she just wanted it for other family members. She had a home that she and my dad had purchased, and maybe she just wanted to get away from there. Anyway, it was a new environment for all of us, and I thought it would be a fresh beginning as well.

While we were living in the apartment, I learned that I was pregnant with my second son. Also, I found out around the same time that my husband was addicted to heroin, and that my new husband had been in and out of prison several times. When I met him, I knew he had just gotten out of prison, and that was intriguing to me. I don't know why? Maybe, I was attracted to the "bad-boy" image, or maybe it was because he was so handsome. Although I had heard about his past, I didn't know that "prison" was a lifestyle for him.

I used to wonder why he would leave early in the morning and come back late at night. Then, I began to understand that the drug had him; his life was not his own but it belonged to the drug. Because I was naïve about street life, I didn't really know what the addiction consisted of or how much it would cost me and my family. I learned real fast that the drug was the most important thing in his life.

Although, my brother Lee had been addicted to drugs, I still wasn't real familiar with the lifestyle. See, Lee was my brother, so he didn't count among other addicts. He was just my brother (if that makes sense).

James didn't take me around to his friends much, but, when he did it was more for "show," like he had won the lottery or something. Because I was naïve, I was just glad to be with him. This one time we met up with someone that we both knew. I had been sleeping with this man prior to the relationship with my husband, and James knew him from the streets.

I guess they got into a conversation about me, and this guy must have made a negative comment. My husband informed him that I was his wife and an argument ensued. I don't know exactly what happened afterwards but I do know it wasn't good. From what I remember, someone got shot.

(I pray he survived, but I never heard anything else about him or the shooting.)

While I was pregnant, we moved to the west side of Detroit, I thought that it would help James get off heroin. That would not be the case.

After I gave birth to our son, James Kennedy Jr. (or Jay Jay), things seemed to get a little better. James now had a son, and he enrolled in a Methadone Program.

I thought that would be the answer and he would get a job and we would live a happy life. Right.

We both eventually began to work for my mother at one of the Home for the Aged facilities that she was the Administrator over. I was a Nurses' Aide, and James worked in maintenance. It worked for about a year, but every day on lunch, he had to go get the Methadone, which became a problem and eventually caused him to lose his job.

My father was diagnosed with colon/rectal cancer when I was around 11 years old. Once he could no longer work, my mother took on a second job as a Pharmacy Tech at a local neighborhood pharmacy.

Now, at this point in my marriage, she got me a job working with her.

As for my husband, we were more off than on. He would be at my home for months, then jump on me—stealing the money, food stamps, or anything he could get his hands on, and he would be on the streets for months. It was like a revolving door. Here a minute, gone a minute.

By this time, my mother had moved into the flat downstairs with my little sister and brother (Beverly and K-Man) and my cousins (Kalm and Money). The children were in daycare, and they were there to help me as well. Things seemed to finally be going well. James had come back home, and things were rocky but we were making it.

I never established a relationship with his family. I think we were civil to each other, tolerated each other, but never had a "relationship." His mother was a woman who looked out for and protected her children, and there was little left for anyone else. I don't know if it was because, before my brother went to prison, he impregnated my husband's sister or something else, but I never felt that she cared for me or my family. I believe she and my mom were the closest, but there was no love for me or my children (even though one of my sons was her biological grandchild and my oldest son called her son "daddy"). Never a "Happy Birthday," "Merry Christmas"—nothing from Grandma K. I don't fault her for any of it; it was what it was. She, like most women who had been abused as well, did the best she could and had given all she had to give.

One particular incident stands out to me because it still hurts, although I have forgiven.

Unfortunately, every time I think about it, the raw emotions of the pain resurface.

We were at his mother's house, without a dime, my children must have been about two and three years old. His mother had walked to the store, and, when she returned, she came back with juice, chips and candy for my nephew (my brother's child) but offered my children nothing. I had to watch my children watch him eat all of his snacks, and I could not offer them anything. She could have put it up for him later or asked him to share with my children, but no. She sat him right at the dining room table and let him eat those chips and that candy. I felt that he was taunting them (like in a "see-what-I got" kinda way).

As I replay that incident in my head, it's like he was eating in slow motion so the kids could watch him eat, all the time asking me for chips and juice. Or, was it just my imagination? I also remember that he was never allowed to play with my children, as if my children weren't "good enough," or had a disease or something.

I don't know what that was really about. Maybe she was just "over protective" of my nephew? Whatever was going on, it made a lasting impression on me.

Memories that I will never forget. Not that I haven't forgiven—but it's still there, stuck in my mind, no matter how hard I try to let it go.

This dark emotional place that I was in was devastating on so many levels. How did I get to a place where I couldn't buy my children a bag of chips and a juice? Better yet, why was I in a relationship with someone who couldn't buy my children a bag of chips or juice? I often wondered, "Lord what am I doing here?" It broke my heart that a mother would do that to children; forget about me, but *why did you have to be so mean or disrespectful to my children*? They were children! They didn't know, and I couldn't offer them anything.

Needless to say, that would be the last time I stepped foot into her house. Not because of them, but for my own peace of mind. You can do what you want and say what you want about me, but don't come after my children. Yes, even thinking about it now, I feel bad, but mostly I feel sorry for her.

I believe she had been so hurt and abused in her past that she only had her children and her grandchild to bring her joy. It saddens me to think that she was incapable of loving others, but that's the way it seemed to me. I would never disrespect my elders, so it was best for me to remove myself, completely.

When James and I first started dating he had given me the nickname "DJ," and everyone began to call me by that name. One particular evening after discussing our dinner plans, it was decided that I would walk the two blocks to the grocery store to pick up some food.

As I walked into the store, a guy was flirting with me, and he asked me my name. I quickly said "DJ," smiled, and kept shopping. I didn't know that James had followed me to the store. I didn't think anything of it and continued to shop. As we were leaving, the gentleman said, "See you later, DJ"— and what did he say that for?

James began to beat me right there in the store parking lot. He hit me in the eye and knocked me on the ground. He beat me so bad that people had to pull him off of me.

Not only was I physically battered, but by now I was emotionally battered as well. The beating seemed to last forever, and the aftermath of it was even worse. My eye was so swollen that at one point the doctors thought that I may lose it; my face and body were all black, purple, green, and blue.

I had taken all that I could withstand, I could take no more. I remember his mother coming to see me after the beating; she told me how to get rid of the bruises quickly: use Witch Hazel. Then she told her son that he shouldn't have beaten me like that. That's all that was said. No "How are you? Can I do anything to help?" Nothing! Really!

This would be the end of our marriage but the beginning of a long battle back.

Although we were legally married for over seventeen years, we were only physically together for about three years. They were the worst and longest three years of my life (or so I thought at the time). Again, I retreated back into myself. I didn't want to return to work. I didn't want to come out of the house. I would not lift up the window shades to let the light in, and I would stay in bed all day while the boys were in school.

Not only was I embarrassed because the entire neighborhood knew about it, but I fell into a deep depression. I just wanted to stay in the safety of my home, with my children. No outsiders allowed, including family.

Trying to make someone else happy left me *BROKEN*.

2. A Time of Peace

After the beating, James and I both agreed that it was time to separate for good. He went on with his life, and I tried to gather myself together and move on with my life. It would take a couple of months, but I finally pulled myself back together and began to live again.

By this time, my focus had changed, and I was trying to do things that would allow me and my sons to have a better life. I started back working at the pharmacy, and now I was enrolled in Wayne County Community College, but I was struggling.

I graduated from high school when I was sixteen. School had never been an issue for me; school was always my "safety net." Learning always exposed me to greater things. I always felt that education was my way out, or my escape. It allowed me to escape to other places in the world, or to think of things other than myself. As I reflect back, I was always eager to learn more. More about the world, more about physical and emotional health. Yes, it was an escape route for me even as a young child. However, I found myself overwhelmed trying to work, go to school, and raise my sons.

It eventually proved too much for me, and I became hospitalized. I knew I couldn't keep going at this pace, and I needed something more. I needed a job with good benefits and pay so that I could take care of my sons without struggling.

Like most girls growing up in my era, I dreamed of being an airline stewardess or nurse. I always saw myself helping people. Unfortunately, because I hated science and math nursing would never work out. Although I didn't doubt that I could do the job, I lacked the confidence to push through college to become a nurse.

But I was good in English and grammar. I could read and write, so I would have to settle for some other career. But what?

My mother was a Tax Preparer, and one of her clients worked at United Airlines. As I was helping my mother one evening, this gentleman asked me what I thought about becoming a Flight Attendant. He had no idea that that was one of my "dream jobs," but, I told him, because I had children, I didn't think I would qualify. He informed me that I was wrong and later brought me an application for the position.

After speaking with my mother, I was discouraged from pursuing this career because I had two children to take care of, and they needed me to be at home with them on a consistent basis. She also didn't want to watch them while I went away for training. I understood and watched the dream die.

Several years later, I was still determined to make a better life for us. I began to see the United States Army "Be all you can be" advertisements. This would be perfect. I would have a great job and good pay; they would pay for my college degree; I would be able to travel, and the boys could come with me. *Perfect!*

I had been thinking about this idea for several months. One day, coming home from school in downtown Detroit, I was tired, weary, and ready to give up. As I was walking to the bus stop, I noticed a Recruitment Center—mind you, I walked this way all the time and never noticed it before now. So, I decided to go in and speak with a recruiter.

I took the test right then and there and was told that I could go into any branch of the armed forces that I decided to go into. However, because I had children, the Army would be the best for me.

I began to listen to the recruiter, and he made everything seem so exciting. He told so many lies, and I was ignorant of the fact that it was a sales job. And, besides, he was flirting with me, and it had been a long time since I had that kind of attention.

I went home and thought about it and talked about it with my mother. She was totally against it, but I didn't believe I had any other options. Either I was going to continue to work like a slave child or try something different. The next time I went to school, I went in and signed the papers.

I committed to the United States Army for four years, and I would be leaving in six months. That would give me enough time to get things in order at home and prepare for me to leave my children for three months (or so I thought).

To celebrate my decision, the recruiter took me to dinner, and I was the dessert. The cycle of sexual promiscuity returned. So, not only did he get a new recruit but he had the luxury of having my body as well, an added bonus. While he was driving me home that night, I thought about how he had just played me. I shrugged it off because I was used to being taken advantage of...

It was normal for me—plus, I would never have to see him again, anyway. All the papers had been signed, and I was on my way to a better future for us.

Unfortunately, not only did he take advantage of me physically but the lies that he told me were tremendous.

For starters, I had made it very clear that I didn't want to be away from my children any longer than necessary. I was assured that I would have six weeks of basic training and another six weeks of advance training (for my particular MOS, or job), then I would go to Kentucky for approximately a year and a half before heading off to Germany. I would be able to go home between training sessions so that the time away wouldn't seem so long. In Kentucky, I would be able to bring my children to live with me.

I reported to the United States Entry Office on September 22, 1981, at the age of 22. Basic Training was challenging, but—although I was a mother and older than most of the people in my platoon—I was determined to make it through.

The training was rough, and we quickly became a team, pulling each other through hard places. Everything seemed to be working out until I had mess-hall duty and was able to speak to some soldiers who had been in the service for a while. That's when I found out about the many lies that I had been told. As I was confronted with some of the truths, I asked to speak to my commanding officer. He separated the lies from the truth, and I was devastated.

Not only was the assignment after graduation inaccurate, but, because of my job title, I would probably be headed to Germany within six months of graduation. And, before I could have the children join me, I would have to go to Germany, get established, get housing, and ask for permission to have my children join me. So it wasn't as open and shut as the recruiter had said. It wouldn't be that easy for us to Move On to our better life. Lies, Lies. Lies.

I was heartbroken and devastated, taken advantage of *again*! Also, by this time, my mother was complaining about the children because she really didn't want to keep them to begin with, so, when I told her this news, she said, "Donna, you need to come home."

After struggling with myself, I made the decision that this was not what I signed up for, and I would have to leave. Fortunately, I was able to gain the ear of my commanding officer and was able to leave on a "general discharge," which means, yes, I was in the Army, but I would not receive any type of benefits from it. Again, I watched another dream die!

3. Rebounding

During the six months of waiting to go into the Army, I continued to work and prepare to leave. One day while waiting on the bus to go to work, a fine brother drove up and asked for directions. Oh, he was so fine! His name was Richard Pullum Sr., and he was from Baltimore, Maryland. He was here in Detroit visiting his sister. We exchanged telephone numbers and went on about our day.

At this time a high-school friend of mine was living upstairs from me (my mother had moved back to her home on the east side to be closer to work). Rick had made such an impact on me that I couldn't wait to get home from work to tell her about this guy I met on the way to work that morning. Before I could get the words out of my mouth, he called—and I was in Love or Lust.

His sister lived only a couple blocks from me, so he and I met up that night. He seemed like a really nice guy. We instantly hit it off and became inseparable. I wanted to be around him, and he wanted to be around me. Before I knew it, he was staying with me more than with his sister and her family.

Beautifully Broken

When I told him I was about to leave for the service, he helped me prepare for the physical part of training. He had been in both the Army and the Navy so he had plenty of experience. He helped me learn to run with endurance. (He was helping me become the "best I could be," right?) He even tried to tell me that what the recruiter told me was not what was going to happen, but I wouldn't listen. I couldn't believe that the recruiter would lie to me like that, he was a soldier! A government official couldn't possibly be lying.

Rick was attracted to my children instantly, and they were very fond of him, too. They loved it when he was there. It seemed like a "good fit," but I was getting ready to go into the service, so my guard was up. It was nice, but I didn't plan on a long-term relationship; I had other plans. We enjoyed the time we had together, and then I was gone, on my way to Basic Training to be a soldier in the United States Army.

Everything was going well until I found out things weren't going the way I had planned back at home.

It surprised me and burdened me to find out that Rick was staying at my house alone with my children while I was away (this also played a big part in my decision to come back home). Although everyone (including my mother) loved him, I didn't know him like that, but my mother must have been overwhelmed with the boys because she allowed it. So he was staying at my house with my children while I was in boot camp, at the time when my mother told me, "Donna, it's time to come home."

It was when I returned home that I began to see the other side of Mr. Pullum. It became obvious that he had a drinking problem, and he was verbally and emotionally abusive. I guess I didn't see the warning signs before because I had no intentions of being with him long term. We were just enjoying the time together before I left. However, by this time, he had moved in and I became committed to trying to make this relationship work. My boys liked him, my mother liked him, my family liked him, so, surely, I had to like him too, right?

As time went on, the drinking became even more excessive, and the abuse escalated to a place of fear.

He would drink, then we would fight; he would cry and ask for forgiveness, and I would forgive, then he would drink and we would fight, cycles! He would also have flashbacks to Vietnam. What was this? Luckily, it only happened when he was drunk: turning over couches, having everyone to be quiet because the enemy was coming. I used to laugh to myself at first; I thought he was faking. But they began to come more often. And after the flashback came the fights.

One fight left me with stitches in my head. His family kept telling me to leave him alone, but he kept coming back, crying and apologizing. He was a great person while he was sober, but, when he started to drink, watch out! He was truly Dr. Jekyll and Mr. Hyde. By this time, I loved him and I wanted to be with him but I wanted/needed him to stop with the drinking. Little did I know that this was nothing compared to what was to come.

I found out that he was also married and had left his wife and son in Baltimore. They were having marital problems, and that's why he was here in Detroit. That didn't bother me at all because, I wasn't trying to get married, and I had a husband somewhere in Detroit as well.

Because he was a veteran it wasn't difficult for him to find work with the federal government. Before leaving the Baltimore area, he had applied at Fort

Meade Army Base. He finally received a call regarding employment back in the Baltimore/Washington area. I was secretly happy because I thought he would leave and the abuse would stop, but he wouldn't go unless I went with him. Still trying to find a better life for me and my sons, I agreed to go with a plan, that in six months I would bring my children down to Baltimore with us. So, again, I picked up and left, headed to Baltimore with someone who had more secrets than even me and my family.

When we arrived in Baltimore, I was introduced to his son (my son), Little Rick, who quickly became my best friend. We stayed in a hotel for a few days until we were able to find a studio apartment on the east side of Baltimore, on 25th St and Calvert.

The street was lined with row houses and businesses. It was my first time seeing a row house, and I was fascinated with the marble steps. Everyone had marble "stoops."

I would sometimes come and sit and just watch the traffic go by, imagining about the drivers' lives, where they were going or what type of job they were leaving.

The neighborhood was mixed racially and economically, both "haves" and "have not's." We had plenty of homeless on the street as well. They were always respectful, though.

It wasn't long before I found a job with a retail pharmacy. The plan seemed to be working out until it wasn't. Before I started working, Rick would come home to dinner and for maybe a walk afterwards, but, once I began to work and I was no longer there when he got home, he started coming home later and later. On pay day I wouldn't see him until late in the evening, and he would be broke.

I was trying to find out what was going on until he finally told me, he had an addiction problem. He was a heroin addict. I thought to myself *Not again!* By this time, the abuse was fierce, and he had instilled so much fear in me that I was scared to do anything other than stay. The one thing that gave me a little glimmer of hope was Little Rick.

I missed my sons so much that I would beg his dad to go get him on the weekends so that I could feel the love of a child. He had become my peace and my protection. And Rick didn't fight me as much when Little Rick was around.

In spite of everything that was going on, I began to focus on providing a place for me and my sons to live. I loved living in Baltimore, and I didn't want to return to Detroit, but I needed my children with me. As a little girl, I always desired to live in another city—anywhere but Detroit! I always felt that I needed to escape from something but could never figure it out.

By this time, the abuse had gotten so bad that he was sending me to the hospital. I went to work with so many black eyes. The last incident, he hit me so hard in my chest that he bruised my sternum and my ribs.

My office manager went to the hospital with me and on our way back she had a "heart-to-heart" talk with me. She was concerned that I would not make it through one of these beatings, and she strongly urged me to return to Detroit.

I called my mother and asked her if she would come and get me. I was headed back to Detroit, again, embarrassed and ashamed.

We had set it up that she would come on Saturday morning. By this time, Rick would usually be out all night on Friday, so, if we timed it right, we could leave without him knowing. I knew he wouldn't let me leave on my own. There would be bloodshed, and I was afraid. Saturday morning would be the perfect time to make my getaway.

However, this particular Friday, he decided to come home, and, by the time my mother arrived, he was there. This was before cell phones, so I couldn't warn her not to come. When he found out I was leaving, he cried like a baby, begging me not to leave.

I got in the car, and he got in the car and refused to get out, so he ended up coming back to Detroit with me. I think both my mother and I were too scared of him to demand that he stay behind. Not only did escape seem impossible, but, again, my dream of a better life away from all the hurt, pain, and secrets that waited on me in Detroit was destroyed.

I eventually went back to work at a retail pharmacy, and he went to work at the Post Office. I thought that he would finally get it together. Unfortunately, that lasted about two months before he got fired because he wasn't focused enough to grasp the job. He was so worried about what I was doing that he couldn't focus. The insane jealousy and the addictions that were operating in his life would not allow him to function. So now I was working, and he was staying home with the children.

This arrangement was working out well; we had been here before. He was the perfect mate when he wasn't drinking. I would come home from work, and the house would be spotless, the children fed, their homework done, and my food and bath ready, it was perfect. All I had to do was work. All he had to do was not drink!

He would be good during the week, but, come Friday night, he would make up for the whole week of being Mr. Mom. He would go out every Friday night. The boys and I would be so glad to see him leave on Friday night; we would laugh, dance, and have fun until we heard the car pull up in the back of the house.

The boys would run and get in their beds and I would play like I was asleep.

It usually didn't matter whether I was asleep or not because he would wake me up with his fist, or with accusations that I had been with another man. When, where, and how did I have time to be with anyone? He held all the cards; he had all the control.

By this time, he had persuaded me to begin taking pills from the pharmacy and selling them. I must admit the money was good, and, with only me working, it helped with a lot of bills, making life a little easier.

As a result of this bad behavior (Lord, if I have not repented before, please forgive me now, in Jesus' Name), I purchased a car that I never drove. *He* took me anywhere I needed to go. He dictated when we were going and when we were leaving. Anything that needed to be done inside or outside of the house, he did it. I went to work and home and maybe to mama's if he was feeling good.

When you are in an abusive relationship, losing your own identity can happen so quickly without you realizing what has actually happened.

I didn't realize it at the time, but I had lost myself. I lost my independence, my ability to think for myself and make my own decisions. I had no desires, no ambitions, no hope. Nothing mattered except trying to make it through the week without a black eye. He had managed to take full control of my (our) lives. While in in abusive relationships, it may take years before you wake up and realize that your life has taken a turn and you have lost yourself. You're now operating in survival mode.

The abuse was so great that my sons didn't want to be there, and I didn't want them there. We made every excuse for them not to be there. They would be at my mother's over the summer or on the weekends. We were all looking for a way out. Things would get so bad that I would have to leave *my house* to get away from him because of his alcohol use and abuse.

As if this wasn't bad enough, we were living during the height of the Crack Cocaine Epidemic, and a family member introduced him to Crack. He was off and running... He even tried to get me "cracked out." His description of how he had gotten his first wife strung out on drugs is etched in my memory.

That thing stung like a bee when he told me that. That he would be that low-down to deliberately try to get me strung out on drugs. I don't know if he said it to be cruel or if he was being honest, but it cut like a knife. Not just for me but for Robin (his wife) as well. (There was one difference between

Beautifully Broken

her and me, though. I kept saying "I don't want to," and she would say, "Let's get high.")

4. The Pregnancy

Crack cocaine took the abuse to a whole different level. One night while "bingeing," he got mad because I would not get high with him and because I didn't have any more money, so he began to beat me with the butt of a rifle. He beat my legs to the point that you could see the imprint of the rifle on my legs, causing my bed to be full of blood.

While we were out on another crack run (this time on credit), the boys woke up to find my bed full of blood. I don't know how they got away from the house, but they were gone by the time we got back, and I was so grateful.

My family eventually came and took me away from there, and I ended up going into a shelter. The shelter sent me to the emergency room where I received stitches and crutches. My legs were badly battered.

While I mended, I enrolled my children in the school system that the shelter was affiliated with. I stayed there for about two months until I left to live with my mother.

It was at this time that Rick went to the Veterans Rehabilitation Center for the first time. I moved back home and tried to regain some sense of a normal life. He came out of rehab after about a month, with no place to go, and I agreed to let him come back to my home. It wasn't so much that I wanted him back, but I felt sorry for him, and I thought he deserved another change. Always trying to help and getting battered and bruised in the process.

Rick developed a bad toothache and needed something for pain. Since I worked in the pharmacy, I brought home some Tylenol with Codeine for him. Before I knew it, I was bringing him more and more Tylenol, but I didn't mind because it kept him from drinking. Unfortunately, I didn't know that he had become addicted to pain pills, and, when he didn't have them, his behavior was three times worse than it was when he drank liquor. The more I brought, the more he took, until once again the abuse became unbearable.

Then, in 1984, I received some news that I was not prepared to hear: "You're pregnant." I remember sitting in Dr. Frankel's office at Northside Medical Center and crying like a baby. I didn't just *cry*; I was weeping from the inside. *Lord, this is the last thing I need.*

By this time, Rick was on his second or third trip from VA Rehab, and was doing well. He had started going to NA Meetings, and I was trying to be supportive. However, I knew that, if I told him I was pregnant, he would never leave me alone. He had talked about having another child. I just didn't think that I would be his child's mother. I didn't want any more children; I was struggling with the two I had, and this relationship was *all* bad. Also, I had previously had several abortions, and I vowed to myself that I would not have another one. I just could not take the emotional pain of another abortion.

As I sat there, Dr. Frankel tried to console me by telling me, "This is your life and your body," but he had no idea what or who I was dealing with.

I remember crying out to God, "Lord what am I going to do?" Scared, just like that "Forgotten Child," not being able to see a way out of this mess that I found myself in, again. But, how could I have a child with this maniac? I kept the news to myself for weeks just trying to work out an exit strategy.

I needed a plan that would allow me to get away or figure out how I was going to live, knowing that a child would bind me to him forever.

I waited until I could not wait any longer, I was beginning to show, and he had already started to sense that something was going on. So, I took a deep breath and informed him that I was pregnant. Lord, help me!

Within a week after I told him about the pregnancy, I began to bleed very heavily. He took me to Sinai Hospital in Detroit, where they informed us that I had lost the baby (a miscarriage) and that they needed to do a D&C, to clean me out.

Immediately, my mind began to think that God was punishing me for my thoughts. How could I not want my child? That really wasn't the case. It's not that I didn't want a child; I just didn't want to be with Rick. There was so much abuse; I just wanted to be free.

Of course, Rick now was drinking again, and, as usual, he was drunk. We were sitting and listening to the doctor's report; Rick sat for about 10 minutes, and then abruptly and loudly instructed me to get dressed because we were leaving.

I was so confused. They were saying I lost the baby, and he was demanding that I leave. Of course, I left, feeling empty and confused.

I wanted my BABY and here they were saying I lost it. Did my reaction to being pregnant cause me to miscarry? A thousand thoughts were going through my mind. I cried all night, not for myself but because I felt guilty, believing I brought the miscarriage upon myself. And then there was Rick, blaming me, claiming that I must have done something to cause this. He had no idea I was already beating myself up because I blamed myself.

The following morning, he took me to Henry Ford Hospital, where they confirmed that, although I was bleeding heavily, I was still pregnant. A wide range of emotions flooded in, and I just cried tears of joy. All the emotions of doom that I had about having this baby quickly went away, and I was so grateful to God that He allowed me to keep my child. From that point, I was happy and grateful about my pregnancy. Well, as happy as I could be because all the problems were still there.

Approximately one year prior to this, (at Rick's urging), I had applied for a pharmacy position at the VA Hospital, and right after finding out I was pregnant, I received an offer for my dream job; a position at VA Hospital in the Outpatient Pharmacy. I was so scared of not being accepted for the job that I didn't tell them I was pregnant until after I got my 90 days in. I had finally gotten a job with benefits, and I didn't want to do anything to lose it.

When I became pregnant, the physical abuse stopped but Rick made up for it in emotional abuse. I remember, before I went on maternity leave, one of the ladies that I was working with at the VA asked me if the baby and I were okay. She said that I didn't seem happy about being pregnant. I assured her I was happy but was going through a lot. She said she already knew it but would be praying for me. I thought I was good at keeping secrets. She told me she would be praying for me, something I really needed to hear. My lack of faith was still evident because I didn't want anything to do with church or God. However, when she spoke it, I greatly appreciated it. The weight of the world seemed to be on my shoulders, and it had been so long since I had been genuinely happy.

The only peace that I did have was with my children, and I always felt as though I was failing them.

As I got further into my pregnancy Rick was very excited and accommodating. I remember craving crabs, and he would drive me all over the city of Detroit looking for Blue Crabs. The craving was so bad I would cry if we couldn't find any. The boys wanted nothing to do with the crabs, though. They would play with them until they were ready to be cooked, and then they would sit on the front porch. It was so funny how they would run out of that house. For me, the crabs were a necessity. (To this day, my daughter, Tiffany, product of that pregnancy, loves crab.) Strange how some situations can seem so terrible but we can always find something to be grateful for.

I kept working at the retail pharmacy on my days off so that I could continue to get and sell the pills. I also needed to be able to keep Rick supplied with his pills. After I came out on maternity leave, I worked at the retail pharmacy full time. I was actually at work when I went into labor. I went to work that morning, went by my mother's after work, and delivered my daughter, Tiffany, that night.

After being off on maternity leave, I returned back to the VA Hospital. However, since I had a baby to care for, I was no longer able to work in the retail pharmacy on my off days, which was all right with me. I didn't like stealing, and I especially didn't like selling drugs. Although I didn't sell them individually but wholesale, I still felt like a drug dealer. I was helping some other family deal with their own "Rick." The VA gave me the perfect excuse to get away from the drug business because of my work schedule. I worked from 11:00 a.m. to 7:30 p.m., which left little time for anything except for caring for my three children.

The hardest part was that now Rick would have to purchase his own drugs. This became costly and intrusive. Everything revolved around him having pills. Pills to wake up on and pills to go to sleep. Once again, Dr. Jekyll and Mr. Hyde would show up.

For those who have never heard of these characters, let me explain: Dr. Jekyll had an alter-ego or another personality—Mr. Hyde. Dr. Jekyll was a kind and respected English doctor who had repressed evil urges inside of him. To hide his secret, he developed a serum that he believed would effectively mask his dark side. However, this serum caused him to turn into Mr. Hyde. Rick's serum was alcohol and drugs. He would be Dr. Jekyll during the week and Mr. Hyde on the weekend. So, on Friday nights, the fights continued.

After another big fight I had had enough. This time I wasn't as tolerant as before. Giving birth to my daughter left me with a feeling of added responsibility. I wasn't so willing to continue being in a "dead-end" relationship. I had my children to look out for. Now that I had a good job, I knew we would be able to make it on our own. Besides, I was paying all the bills anyway. I would just have to find a sitter. This relationship had to end; I could not and would not continue to be abused. Rick Pullum Sr., had to go, now!

5. Relocating

I believe Rick's family convinced him to return to either Baltimore or Washington, DC. He ended up going to Washington, DC, and started working for the federal government again. It seemed as if his life had been placed back on the right track as well.

He contacted me and asked if he paid for our plane fare, if I would bring Tiffany down to DC for her second birthday. *Absolutely!* I could use a free vacation.

This trip turned out to be the first of many that we took to DC to visit him and so he could see Tiffany. He absolutely adored her. It was during one of these weekend trips that he asked me about moving to the DC area. I'd always wanted something more than what Detroit offered me, and it didn't take much to encourage me to leave. I knew better, but I was so desperate to find something new—a fresh start. I wanted to be somewhere that people did not know me. I did not want to have to worry about my past problems or mistakes anymore, no judgment. I yearned for something more and this was my opportunity.

It took over a year of weekend trips to DC before I allowed him to convince me to move. Our agreement was that, if he could prove to me that he wasn't drinking and could locate and rent a place for me and the kids to live then, I would consider moving there. I loved living in Baltimore when I was there, I liked visiting DC, and so I was excited but cautious.

When he secured an apartment for us in Riverview, MD (a suburb of DC) I was pleasantly surprised. He had to be doing things right because the old Rick would not have been able to hold onto the money long enough to be able to get a three-bedroom apartment for us to live in. I was determined that I would not leave my children again, so it had to be large enough for all of us. What I didn't know was that it would be in a high-crime, income-based housing area and that many secrets were about to be exposed.

I was able to transfer my position from Detroit VA to the Washington, DC, VA Hospital, so I made the move. Although my mother pleaded with me not to go, my sister and I loaded up a U-Haul van, piled the furniture and the kids up in the back, and we were off to Maryland, determined to make a new life for us.

Upon arrival, it didn't take long before my sister and I both realized that again I had been deceived. *Here I go again*, I thought; I was trying to "wish" things into existence. I wanted things to work out so badly. I wanted to live in Maryland. I wanted it to work out between Rick and me. I wanted a family, and I wanted to be happy. Dang, was that too much to ask?

Although things weren't the way he portrayed them to be, I had made the move by then—too late to turn around now. It lasted about two months!

The one smart thing that I did before leaving Detroit was to have a conversation with my boss. I asked my boss at the Detroit VA if he would try to hold my position for a few months so that, if things didn't work out, I would have a job when I got back, and he quickly agreed. I Thank God for Favor.

My sister was reluctant to leave, but I knew she couldn't stay with me forever, so I sent her back home on the Greyhound as I tried to settle into a new lifestyle. I would soon begin working at the Washington, DC, Veterans Administration Hospital.

I had gotten the kids settled in school, and Tiffany was in daycare. In spite of a rocky start, it was coming together, or so I hoped.

But, no matter how much I tried to deny it, the secret was out: the drinking had never stopped! Instead of trying to hide it, Rick quickly began coming home from work drunk. The verbal and physical abuse was soon to follow. It wouldn't be long before we were back in the same place. He would come in from work drunk and start fights, fussing and cussing all the time. Nothing was ever right, and it was always my fault. The children and I had such a good time when he wasn't there and were on pins and needles when he was home. Again, the weekends became a time of terror and dread.

I had been showing up to work with black eyes and bruises, and a gentleman whom I worked with pulled me to the side and offered one of his homes for me to rent so that I wouldn't have to return to Detroit. However, I knew that this would never work. Rick would not allow me to stay in Maryland and not be with him. I didn't want to bring anyone else into this mess that could possibly cost someone their life.

Although my relationship with this gentleman had been strictly platonic, I didn't want to enter into any more-intimate type of relationship, and I didn't want to feel obligated so I declined the offer.

The apartment complex we lived in was huge, and it wouldn't be long before I found out that the boys were writing to my mother, begging her to come get them. They were afraid! There had been a murder at the complex, and a body was found not far from our apartment building. I knew within myself that we wouldn't be living there much longer.

I tried to make it work; I wanted it so badly—though I don't know if I actually wanted the relationship to work or if I just didn't want to come back to Detroit. Another "I told you so," another "feeling trapped," and another "failure." Yet, it was undeniable we were headed back home.

I had brought a pistol with me because I was determined not to allow myself to go through what I had encountered in Detroit. The boys and I would hide the pistol (unloaded of course) in different spots so Rick couldn't find it.

The last straw came one night when he had come home from work drunk, as usual. We had dinner and put the kids to bed, all the while he continued to drink. When we went to bed, I was determined not to have sex because he had been verbally abusing me all night. I had just had enough, and I couldn't take it anymore, so I said no.

As much as I was determined to not have sex, he was much more determined that he would not be denied, so he raped me, over and over again throughout the night! He had his way every way possible, and all I could do was cry. When he finally passed out, I lay there, broken. This was it; if I couldn't stop him from abusing me, I was ready to put us both out of our misery. I was willing to go to jail for killing him, but he would not get another chance to hit me or emotionally abuse me. It was going to stop, tonight! I lay there for what seemed like an eternity, planning the murder. I was so numb, and, because I didn't want to wake him, I lay there in the blood and semen from being raped.

I envisioned myself going into the front-room closet, getting my pistol, putting the bullets in the chamber, walking over to the bed, placing the gun barrel at his left temple, and pulling the trigger. Then I would call the police and tell them to come get me. For over two hours as I lay there and cried, I saw myself doing this.

I gave no thought that I would be in jail in Maryland, I gave no thought that the state may have had the death penalty for first-degree murder. I felt like a zombie.

It took all that I had in me (and God's hand of protection over me) to keep me from committing murder. The one and only thing that stopped me from taking his life was I knew that I would go to jail and my kids would be going into the system. Who would take care of my kids?—we were in Maryland with no friends or family. The thought of my three children being placed into the Foster Care System shook me back to life, and I began to make plans to leave the next morning, early. We would have to do it quickly, so I began to pray to God that he would go to work and not stay home. I would not or could not stay another night. This was it; it was over!

So, instead of committing murder, I got up and quickly got him off to work as usual. Then I hurried and got myself together. I woke the boys and told them to start packing what they could. Then, I dropped my daughter off at daycare because he had a habit of calling and checking on her. It was only by the grace of God that I found a taxi driver who was willing to take me into Washington, DC, to pick up my check, take me to cash it, wait for us to pile whatever belongings we could get, and then take us to the Greyhound Bus Station.

I was so terrified waiting in the bus station, scared that Rick was gonna find out that we left and scared that he would find us. When we boarded that bus, I knew we would be all right! We came home with nothing, but we had our lives!

Once at home I began the rebuilding! I hadn't filed taxes for over three years, so I got my mom to file my taxes. As I waited on my refund to come, we stayed with her. So much had happened—I didn't want to go back into my house the way I had left it. I needed "new," and I thought a coat of paint and some new furniture would provide that. (I had taken and left all of my furniture in Riverview, MD). What I didn't realize was that I needed a new "change of mind." A fresh coat of paint or carpet cleaning could not wash away the frustration and hurt of abuse. Only God could heal this pain.

Before leaving for Maryland, I had begun attending church. Not that I was trying to be "saved," but I knew I needed something more in my life. I had grown up around church, but I was still mad at God for allowing my father to die. Also, due to the abuse

I'd suffered at the hands of the Pastor, I didn't feel that God really loved me the way everyone was trying to say that He did.

See, if God was the all-powerful, all-knowing, all-loving God and was so great, then how could He allow my dad to die at such a young age—especially when I, at the age of 15, needed him most? And, how could He allow a representative of His to sexually abuse me in that manner?

I struggled with those thoughts for a long time, but I wanted my children to know God. I knew it was the right thing to do, even if there was so much I didn't understand. But, when I came back from Maryland, I fell again into the trap of not wanting anything to do with the church or God because once again I was hurt, used, and abused. Where was God in this?

I'm so grateful that I had the insight to ensure that I could return to my position at the VA Hospital.

I quickly readjusted and began to pull my life back together again. It took a lot of humility and determination for me to get on with my life. I felt that I had been trapped and living a lie for far too long. It was time to live.

This time, I was determined that I would not develop any long-term relationships. I wanted nothing to do with being tied down to any one person. I didn't intentionally set out to keep men at a distance, but I wanted nothing to do with them outside of getting some sexual satisfaction—and *I* would determine with whom, when, where, and how I got it. We could see each other, have fun and go about our lives. No attachments, period.

Within six months of our return home, a big surprise came knocking on my door...

6. He's Back

I finally began to get comfortable after returning home from Maryland. I had left the house in shambles, so it would take a couple of weeks to get it in order for us to move back in. I am grateful that I had men in my family who were capable of putting things back in order while I worked on re-establishing our life's plans.

Finally, I was able to return home. When I did, I was able to go and get my goddaughter, Nekita. I had left her in Michigan with my brother because she had already experienced so much pain and turmoil in her young personal life that I didn't want to take her to Maryland when I didn't know what I would be getting myself into. I thought that, once we got things in order, I would send for her or come and get her. As it turned out, leaving her behind was for the best, because one of us would probably have killed Rick while we were in Maryland.

After several months we began to love our lives again when—all of a sudden—the enemy reemerged on my doorstep.

Here was Rick, the one who beat me, the one who raped me, the man that made me flee from

Maryland with the clothes on my back and my children in tow. How dare he come to my house and have the audacity to knock on my door. Drunk as usual. What did he want? Why was he here?

I reluctantly opened the door and asked him those very questions. His voice took on a peculiar tone; he sounded as if he were a baby, looking for love. He had been wounded in the process, too. I could see it in his eye, but I didn't want to see the hurt and the pain. He'd hurt *me*! Why did he have to come back? He had a good job at Walter Reed Army Base; why couldn't he have stayed there?

He had lied, cheated, and connived to get me to move to Maryland. I lost everything; my house full of furniture, my pride, my dignity, my self-respect, all because of him. Then he had the nerve to come back and knock on my door like I was supposed to be happy to see him. *Get away from me!*

But my heart would not allow me to treat him the way I wanted to, I wanted to turn my back on him; I wanted to hate him for the things he had done;

I wanted to destroy him as a man the way that he had destroyed me, but my heart wouldn't let me.

So like a fool, I let him back into my home, but *not* into my life! That part was over; it was done, finished. I would never allow him to get that close to me again. I needed to keep my distance; I needed to develop a "friend" relationship with him, if that was possible. That's the only way I could deal with him.

Rick had a way of showing up—not calling, just showing up. Anyway, this one day he showed up, drunk as usual, when it was just me and Nekita at home. He thought that he was going to fight me the way he used to. But we had news for him.

Nekita and I hemmed him up in the vestibule of the house, and we were getting ready to fight him, to beat him the way he had beaten me so many times before. I wanted to lay the same kind of beating on him that he had done to me numerous times before. But I couldn't. I wish I could have beaten him with the butt of a rifle (as he had done to me). I wish I could have caused him to get stitches in his head (as he had done to me). I wanted to send him to the hospital, broken, bruised, and battered—but I couldn't.

So, instead we threatened to whip his behind, and we allowed him to leave, then Kita and I laughed all day about it. Even as I think about it now, I wish I would have had the strength to fight back because I realized that it wouldn't have taken much to take him down. After all the hell he put me through, when he was confronted, he cowered like a little baby. If only I had known that the roaring lion had no teeth.

We had another incident that would change the course of our relationship. By this time, I had begun my new life, I had returned to work at the VA Hospital; we were back at home; the kids were back in school; and we were trying to get back to life. By this time, Rick had started showing up on a weekly basis.

On one of these days I was with a friend, and we were leaving my house, so I told Rick he had to leave. He had gotten an apartment, and I agreed to drop him off at his home because I didn't want anything to happen to him in his drunken state. As I was driving him home, he called me "bitch" from the back seat. *What—how dare you?* All the hatred and animosity came rushing back.

I stopped the car in the middle of Winthrop Street, pulled out my little .22 pistol, and told him to get out of the car.

Beautifully Broken

I had pulled my pistol so fast that it scared me, because I was ready to shoot him in the head, right in the middle of the street. I made him get out of the car immediately. My friend, who was in the car with us, pleaded with me not to shoot him as he begged and asked for my forgiveness. I did eventually take him home because he was so drunk but ended up leaving him on the curb in the front of his apartment. After that incident, he never came to me wrong again. It was always respectful and apologetic.

By this time, Tiffany was in the fourth or fifth grade. Unfortunately, the older children had left home, and it was just Tiffany and me. I always felt bad because she was a latchkey kid. All the other children always had someone there, both in the morning and afternoons. Unfortunately, Tiffany had to get herself up and ready for school.

I had worked it out where she would go to a neighbor's in the morning, and they would let her ride with them. Since Rick wasn't working, he began waiting for our daughter Tiffany to get out of school, and he would come back and stay at my house with her until I got off of work. At first, I didn't really like this arrangement, but we all benefited from it. It gave them time together, and I knew that she would be safe until I got home from work. Fortunately, by this time Rick and I had learned to become friends. We understood each other, knew each other's likes and dislikes, and boundary lines had been established. We were actually better friends than lovers.

The strange part is that he would come to my house with his girlfriends and try to beat them up, at my house. I couldn't understand his logic. Why did he think it was all right for him to do this? I spoke to several of his female friends and asked them to please leave him alone. I don't think I ever acknowledged all that he had done to me, but I warned them about his behavior. Some listened and some didn't.

I could have held onto all the hurt and pain that he brought into my life, but I made a conscious decision to forgive. Not just for him but for myself and my children as well. See, every child needs both parents, and I never wanted to let what we had been through interfere with my daughter's relationship with her father.

I had already made that mistake before and didn't want to repeat it again. Terry and Jay both loved Rick as well. He had been in their lives from childhood. They knew Dr. Jekyll and Mr. Hyde, the good and bad. Rick had a big heart when he wasn't being controlled by his own personal demons. Yes, a lot of his problems were a result of secrets as well.

7. New Life, New Problems

Once I returned home from Maryland, my life took on some drastic changes. Yes, things seemed to be getting better on the surface, but on the inside I was a wreck. Things are not always what they seem.

I was now raising four children as a single parent with one income. Life was hard, and bills were always due. We had many days and nights with no electricity or gas. It was always one or the other. I tried my best to keep up with the bills, but there never was enough to make ends meet. Poverty has a way of causing havoc in the home, havoc that we are not prepared for. I don't care how careful you are, the "world" has a way of grabbing our children even before we know what's going on.

I had two teenagers in high school, one child in middle school, and one in Kindergarten. My plate was full, and I didn't know how to cope. By this time, my family was the only one in the two-family flat. The boys had the upstairs and we had the downstairs. My sons would always navigate their way to the east side where my mother stayed. I didn't really know why, yet.

One particular day, I received a call from Jay's school informing me that he had been caught with a gun in his backpack and that he would be suspended from school. I was in total shock. My son carrying a gun? How did he get it and why? I was so embarrassed and disappointed. *After everything that we've been through, you decide to take a gun to school?*

Looking back on it, I guess I shouldn't have been so surprised, since I'd had them help me hide a gun from Rick in Maryland. But I had been doing the best I could; I was trying to live a good life in front of them; no men were allowed around them; and I didn't go out a lot. I thought I was making a good impression (the best I could at that point, at least).

What I didn't know was that Jay was being bullied at school by some gang members. He never said a word. Also, I didn't know that, when my sons went to the east side, they had access to *everything*: Drugs, guns, money—everything that young black males did not need in their lives.

Jay wasn't like Terry; he was more reserved and quiet. You never knew what he was thinking or what he was going through because he never spoke of it (secrets took over his life as well, just like mine). Anyway, I found myself as a single mother of four children, raising them in poverty (as one of the working poor), and they were hiding secrets, so many secrets.

Needless to say, Jay was arrested and placed in juvenile detention. I had to go see my son, who was in jail at 13 or 14 years old. It broke my heart each time I went to see him, although I was very thankful that I could see him and no one got hurt.

This placed us in the "youth-correction system," and, although my home had been recognized as a "good" home, we still had to deal with the probation department. His probation officer was very handsome and knowledgeable about "at-risk youth" and how they migrate through the criminal-justice system. He tried to tell me that Jay was headed for trouble, but I wouldn't listen. Not my son! "We have struggled through some hard times so I know he will make better decisions in the future."

Oh, how I wish I would have listened. The officer started coming by and speaking with Jay without appointments and, before you knew it, he and I started talking.

Yes, he was very handsome, but we both agreed to put the brakes on our relationship before we took it any further. I needed someone who was totally focused on my son—and not because he wanted to sleep with me.

The next time I saw him, Jay had transitioned over to adult corrections, and we were headed to a court appointment. All I could do was speak and put my head down as he gave me that "I told you so glance."

I began to have a hard time at work as well, because of all the things that were going on at home, countless court dates and evaluations. Not only was I dealing with Jay's issues but by this time Terry had also begun to stay on the east side more.

It wouldn't be until years later that I found out that my brother had allowed the boys to sell drugs. Since I couldn't give them the things that they wanted or desired, they began to sell drugs for the money. Terry, too, would begin to get caught up with drugs, starting a vicious cycle of drug cases, court, and probation. Mind you, this was in the late 1980s, so the crack epidemic was alive and thriving in the black community.

I had Terry and Nekita enrolled in a high school that could be accessed from either the east or west side, so getting to school was never a problem. When Jay started going to the same high school, the problems of bullying resurfaced.

Terry and Jay had been expelled from school for fighting, and I had to have a conference with the school principal before they would be allowed back to class. While I was in the office waiting on our appointment, the two of them decided to visit some boys in the locker room. Jay started a fight while I was waiting to meet with the principal. That was it—kicked out of school permanently. While they felt that they had to get back at the boys who had been messing with Jay, I was left in the principal's office in the blind. I left the building as tears rolled down my face. The feeling of frustration and defeat rested heavily on me.

One of the ways that I began coping with this stress of kids and bills was to drink. I know the very thing that infiltrated my relationship with Rick is the very thing that I started to consume, more and more.

I was at work one day at the VA and happened to meet a nurse who was experiencing some of the same problems that I was dealing with. We quickly became friends and drinking buddies. I remember the first time I visited her home I began calling her children my nieces and nephews, and they continue to be a part of my life to this day.

The drinking got out of control, quickly. We would drink almost daily after work and especially on weekends. It became "my escape," and I tried to escape, every day! However, I remained functioning, or so I thought. I would often go to work hungover from our get-togethers of the night before. We drank because of "men " problems; we drank because of bills; we drank because of work; we drank and we drank.

When I look back, I can see that we both were running, trying to escape from the hurt, pain, and discontent of our lives. We loved our children with everything we had, but they were driving us crazy. She had two boys and a daughter, and I had two boys and a daughter (all teenagers), and Tiffany was the youngest, the baby. Her children were around the same ages as my older children, so they were good matches. The kids hung out, and we hung out.

Although I had already outgrown the need to go out to bars and clubs, if there was any occasion for our family to get together, I was there. Shoot, we didn't need a special occasion—anything would do. Children's birthday parties always turned into an adult party. Saturday night on the east side was always a reason to get drunk—to go to the park, drunk.

I was reminded of how I had to have Nekita drive us home one night because I was too drunk to do so and too foolish to stay at my mom's. I thank God that He covered me even in the midst of my mess. I would often stay at my mother's house on Saturday night, but, for whatever reason, this particular night I chose to go home. It breaks my heart when I think of all that I have put my children through because of my choices, but I thank God for "restoration"—for allowing me to change and allowing my children to see the change, It was only by the grace of God.

8. Mister Fox

It was during one of those "drunk" weekends in 1989 that I noticed a car driving beside me. The children were at my Mother's, and I was headed home to get ready for work the next morning. Quickly, I became aware of the vehicle at the traffic light beside me, when I turned to look; I saw the driver was trying to get my attention.

This guy was fine and driving a Mercedes Benz. *Wow!* He had me at first sight! I looked at him, and he looked at me and told me to pull over. Mind, you, I had NEVER done anything like this, but he caught me at the right time, and I was all in. When we began to talk, I also noticed that he had a drink too, good!

We began to talk on the phone, and he quickly won me over when I told him my son's birthday was coming up and that I didn't have anything to give him. He brought me $50 the next day, I was amazed. The thought that someone who did not really know me would care enough, to ensure that my son would have a birthday gift meant so much to me. So, I thought, "What's the harm in giving him a shot?"

Mind you, I was seeing people at the time, but it was mainly a money relationship. Understanding, you can prostitute yourself without standing on a street corner.

Remember, I told you that I wasn't interested in any "relationships," so I'd come to see or meet a guy, and we'd make the exchange. At the time, I didn't see the transaction for what it was; I considered it "paying the bills"—and, yes, I would do something a little strange for some change, I didn't think I had any other option.

And, even with him, I didn't want a "relationship" but someone to spend some time with. However, I was willing to allow this guy to meet my family. For me, that was a Big Deal because I had a "motto": *You may spend time with me, but you are not able to meet the kids, brothers, sister, nobody. You deal with me, only.*

When Mr. Fox would come over, I would always make sure we had something to drink. And then we would get drunk. I remember I would make him take "shots" or drink real fast, and we would both get drunk really fast then make passionate love.

I don't know how it managed to work out that way, but very rarely did he come over when the kids would be home. On school nights, Tiffany would usually be asleep.

What I didn't know is that he had secrets of his own. I had noticed that he would jump up and leave quickly. This began to puzzle me—made me ask about a wife and children—and he came clean: he was married and had children. *Wow!* How could you be spending this much time with me and have a family? Why are you here?

Unfortunately, the fact that he had a family fell right in line with my agenda. Remember, I didn't want a relationship. Since he was married, that meant he could go home to his wife and leave me alone. There was just one problem with that: he wouldn't leave me alone.

The more we began to hang out, the more of my family he met, and, before I knew what was going on, I was in a relationship that I didn't want to be in. See, I was still seeing other people, and I thought that would keep me from getting too close to him.

As we began to get closer, he began to try and figure out where I would be when I wouldn't answer the phone at home. Or why the kids would say I wasn't at home (this was before cell phones). Many times, I would be sitting at home or drinking with my girlfriend and didn't want to be interrupted, trying to keep him at bay. Unfortunately, the more I tried to keep him away, the harder he pressed.

Then beepers began to become accessible, and, before I knew it, he had purchased me a beeper. Little did he know that I would cut that beeper off so that he couldn't catch up with me. We had little codes that he would put in with our telephone number to say "Call me," "Where you at?", "Love you," "F___k you!" We had a code for everything. It still makes me laugh when I think back about it. I did everything to run this guy away, but God had other plans.

Once I stopped running, our relationship became serious, but I could not give up my whole heart. There was too much hurt there. I could give you a part of me, but I still held on to the very thing that every relationship needs to survive, my heart! I could only allow you to have a piece of my "me."

My heart was too fragile. It had been broken, crushed, stepped on, used, and bruised so much in the past that I was unreachable when it came to surrendering to Love. I was comfortable with being in Lust, but being in Love was totally out of the question!

Just to set the record straight, let me share this because it has never been told. After approximately six months of dating, I found out that Mr. Fox was married. As I stated previously, this wasn't a problem for me. Non-committal relationships were what I had come to expect and desire. Also, I too was married. It's just that I had no idea where my husband was. We had been separated for many years, and I felt no need to get divorced. I had no plan to marry anyone, so I didn't bother him and he didn't bother me. It worked for me; it kept me safe (or so I thought).

Anyway, once I found out Cornell was married, I tried to break it off with him, but he would not leave me alone, and explained to me that his marriage was over and had been over for some time, so my position was okay. See, whereas I had been imagining that dating a married man meant "No commitment, no obligation; just have a good time and then both go to our separate homes," it didn't work out that way, and I (we) fell in love.

My life had been spiraling out of control. The drinking was quickly taking over my life. I was now drinking every day, going to bed with a drink. I never got to the point where I had to wake up to a drink, and for that I am truly grateful.

Due to this new relationship (which I didn't want), my partying had slowed down tremendously. Cornell would even go out with me to protect me from being an embarrassment to him and myself, always serving as the designated driver because I would be wasted, even though I thought I always presented myself as a lady. How do you do that drunk?

Things with my children had gone from bad to worse. My oldest son had moved out; my middle son was dividing his time between home and the east side; my goddaughter was beginning to spend a lot of time away from home as well. This left just Tiffany and me.

I remember coming to the realization that I was out of control one night when I had returned home from my girlfriend/sister's house.

As I lay in bed, the room was spinning, and I kept calling for Tiffany to come and help me. I distinctly remember her going into the living room where my son was playing his video games and asking him to come and help mama. His reply to her was "Aww, ain't nothing wrong with her; she just drunk."

I may have been drunk, but that shook me to my core. For my child to look at me as a drunk was heart wrenching. I don't know why this bothered me so much, I knew they probably thought it—but actually hearing it showed me "me," and it wasn't good! Also, there, were demons from my past that were trying to resurface and I couldn't allow them to overtake me.

I knew it was time to do something, but what?

Earlier in this book, I spoke about going to church. I had started attending this church with two ladies I worked with at the VA Hospital, Barbara and Brenda (withholding last names). While all of this was happening in my life, I learned that one of the deacons that I loved at the old church had become a Pastor and had started a church of his own. I loved Leon and Gloria Glover! I loved them at the old church and I felt safe with them "emotionally."

Barbara and Brenda had been inviting me to church, but I always found an excuse to get out of attending. Barbara had taken an early retirement, but Brenda and I still worked together, and she stayed on me continuously about coming to church. Even Pastor Leon and Gloria Glover would send messages for me to come to church.

I kept coming up with excuses. Any and every excuse that I could imagine, I gave. Sometimes lies and sometimes truth—if there was anything that I could say to get out of it, I said it. I think deep down inside I knew that, if I stepped into the church building, my life would drastically change, and, although it was rough, I wasn't sure I was ready to go the way of salvation. I had been down that "church" road before, and, although I trusted the leaders, I don't think I was ready to deal with "church folk," not yet.

Through all of this, I knew one of my friends was going through a very difficult time in her life. I would watch her without her knowing it.

I watched how she handled herself on the job, how she handled the stress that I knew she had to be under, and how, even though she was going through some really rough times, it didn't seem that it was affecting her life or her happiness. As I observed her, day in and day out, I didn't quite know what she had, but, whatever it was, I wanted it. I soon discovered that what she had was Jesus.

Then, on a Thanksgiving Day, in 1990, I no longer could come up with an excuse. Pastor Leon Glover had decided to have a Thanksgiving Day service, and we were not working overtime at work (I used this excuse a lot to get out of coming to church). So I wouldn't be working any overtime, and everyone who knew me knew that I spent every holiday at Mama's house, so I wouldn't be cooking (I didn't cook much anyway). The service was early enough so as not to interfere with everyone's holiday plans, and it was going to be a brief service.

Needless to say, I had finally hit a brick wall—"no more excuses!" The game that I played with myself was over. It was time to go to church, Charis Cathedral under the leadership of Pastor Leon Glover. My life would never be the same.

9. A Changed Life

As I prepared us to go to church, something felt different. There was an excitement in my spirit and a dread as well. Although I knew the members from our old church, I didn't know who would be there and if I would be accepted. Besides, it had been years since I had seen or even spoken to them. I was only in contact with Barbara and Brenda. I remember being really nervous.

Church service was good! Praise and worship was good. I had always liked praise and worship.

When the service was just about to finish, I heard the words that I didn't want to hear: "Sister Donna can I pray with you"?

I wanted to scream *"NO!"* I wanted to run to the door. I wanted to escape the way I had done all of my life, but how do you say no to prayer?

My life was in shambles; my life was a mess. I know I needed prayer, but I wasn't ready. I felt that I had done so much that I was disqualified from God's forgiveness and love. Remember, I was supposed to be mad at God.

Beautifully Broken

How could He forgive me? I held on to all of my secrets, and my life was a wreck.

As I was approaching the altar, my heart was saying "Yes," but my mind was saying "No, not today. I can receive salvation some other day." I had rehearsed it all in my mind: I would come back later, another time, and give my life to Christ. I was just visiting today, and I didn't want to let go of my pain.

How crazy is that? My life was a wreck; my children were out of control; I was struggling financially; and I didn't want to let it go. I was holding on to sin as though my life depended on it.

Instead of running out the door the way I wanted to, all I could say was "Yes."

I didn't find out until years later that this was the first time that Charis Cathedral had held Thanksgiving Day service and that it was strangely set up by God, to save my life. I can't say for sure if they ever had another service on that holiday, but I know that it was definitely set up for me. That's the kind of God I serve!

As First Lady Glover began to pray for me, I could feel the weight of the world being lifted off of my shoulders, and I just began to cry. I cried and I cried, and I cried and I cried. I remember reciting the sinner prayer, inviting Jesus into my life, and I cried some more.

It had been so long since I actually cried. With so much going on in my life, I just couldn't cry. The wall that had been built didn't allow me to cry. I just took one punch after another, and I kept it moving. No time to cry, no time to feel the pain, no time to give in to all of my insecurities and emotions. I did as I had been taught as a young girl (The Forgotten Child). You deal with it; you act as if it didn't happen, and you keep moving.

So, for me to actually cry, it took a lot out of me. I didn't really understand exactly what was going on, but I knew that I had been changed and my life would change. That, I was sure of! I could hear this person crying out to God, "Yes Lord, Yes!" This couldn't be me—remember I wasn't ready to give my life to Christ. But this hurt, battered, misguided woman was crying and saying Yes to God, and it felt good.

As I left the altar, I knew that what I had just experienced was exactly what I needed. For some reason, I felt Hope. Hope that my life would be better, Hope that my children would be better, and a Hope for a future. Not just walking through life but actually enjoying life.

I was excited and scared at the same time. *Where do I go from here, what do I do now?* The level of freedom that I felt on that day is something that I hadn't felt in a long time. I realized that my life was worth it and God loved me even in the shape that I was in. Pastor Leon and First Lady Glover had loved on me so much during that service, and I can actually say I felt the love of God running through them and me.

Years later, Pastor Glover would tell me that, when I first walked into that church, my countenance was as black as the bottom of his shoe because of all the sin that was in my life.

I decided to acknowledge this day, this Thanksgiving Day, as my spiritual birthday. A day of new birth, my spiritual birth—and, every year when Thanksgiving comes around, I also thank God for my second birthday.

As I was leaving, I remember Pastor Glover giving me instructions (as most Pastor's do). "Now that you have given your life to Christ, make sure you come back to church and come to Bible Study, and it's important for the children to come as well."

I made a commitment to myself that I would definitely be coming back. Things began to make a little more sense to me. I could actually see myself being free. I went home a different person. No, not that I had changed in the natural but something indescribable had happened to me, and it felt so good. I knew that my life would change, but it would take a while before that would happen.

We began to attend church on a regular basis, My children and I always felt better when we came out.

However, I wasn't really ready to totally commit, not yet. I would come to church on Sundays but party throughout the week. My friend Wilda and I would continue to drink, but now we began to talk about God more. She knew more than I did because she had been a part of a church while she was married. So, many times our conversations would turn to questions about God, and, the more I went to church, the more I could see my life changing right in front of my eyes.

I started inviting everyone to come to church with me, even while I was still drinking. I was telling people about my church, my Pastor and First Lady. Still drinking, still fornicating, still in sin, I just wanted everyone to know Jesus.

Many times, I would try not to go to church, but, when I didn't go, I felt such emptiness inside. I didn't know it at the time, but, for me at that point in my life, I needed to go to church, I needed to be in the presence of the Holy Spirit. Yes, as a mature Christian now, I know that the church is within us, but at that time God was in the church, and I needed to be there.

I was so happy, and it seemed as if the people that I used to hang out with were starting to feel the way I felt. Little did I know that some of my friends had given their lives to Christ and were trying to live for him as well, but we still struggled with our demons of the past. I would still hang out through the week, go to Bible Study on Thursday, and be drunk on Friday and Saturday.

However, on Sunday morning, no matter how "hungover" I was, I made it to church. It was as if I had to be there, but I still did a lot of hitting and missing. One Sunday, I would be there, and then I would miss one, then come for three and miss two.

It was good that I was coming, but it wasn't enough, I had to make a drastic change. One particular incident stands out to me. Every Sunday our family went to Big Ma's house for dinner. There was no particular time to come, but, at some point in the day, we made it there. This particular Saturday I had stayed at Big Ma's house because I had been hanging out. I was sleeping on the floor, and, when I woke up that Sunday morning, I jumped up in a panic because I was going to be late for church.

I remember my mother asking me, "Why do you run to that church all the time," and I couldn't explain it to her. All I knew was that I needed to be there. It was on that day; I realized my life and the things that I had done changed. I jumped up and ran from the east side of Detroit to the west side so that I could attend church. I was late, but I made it.

As time went on and I continued to hit and miss church, one of my best friends and "get-high" buddies got killed on the side of her house. I went through some deep depression after her death, because she had dedicated her life to God like me and was attending church trying to get her life together. I couldn't understand that we can be saved and bad things can still happen to us. I was heartbroken, and I wondered if God really cared. She loved God just as I did; she was going to church just like me; she was trying to leave her past behind, just as I—but she died. Someone killed Shawn Bonner, and I held God responsible.

While we were at the cemetery, I remember the late Bishop Steve Bennett (he was a Pastor at that time) calling me over to his car and giving me a prophetic word. He said, that there was a "spirit of depression over my life" and that I had to shake it off before it consumed me.

I continued to attend church—more hitting and missing, but I knew that I could not completely turn back to my past. There was something about Jesus that I needed. He made my life so much easier.

A few months later, another friend (a "get-high" buddy) got killed. *Lord, what is going on?* I remember being so distraught that I went to my Pastor, because I couldn't understand why God was allowing all of this to happen to my friends. The words that my Pastor spoke to me that day "changed my life, for good."

Pastor Leon Glover said, "Daughter, God will close the door to your past" to allow you to become the woman of God that He has ordained you to be. *Wow!*—this knocked me off my feet. See, these two people who had died held on to some of my secrets that I still can't share (it's not the time), and they took them to their graves. To say that that was a "True Word from God" is an understatement. Those words cut me like a knife, but I knew that they were true, and a Word from the Lord. It was around September or early October that I received this Word, and it was then I decided to live for Christ.

My birthday is in late October, and, following that life-changing Word, I asked my family to come to church with me instead of us partying. We could all go to church and then come to Big Ma's for dinner.

I was so amazed when all of my family showed up at church. My sister, brother, nieces, nephews— every one of them was there. They filled up one section of the church. My heart was overjoyed. Not only did they come to church, but they accepted Jesus into their lives. My entire family! And they kept coming every Sunday. Before I knew it, they were attending on a regular basis as well. God is so good!

I really began to desire more of God. I was at church every Sunday, at Bible Study every Thursday with my children. They liked being there, I loved to be there. Good things were happening for us, finally. It was customary for whoever was teaching Bible Study to ask if everyone had found the scripture, and we would laugh amongst ourselves because we always had to answer with a "Please wait."

It actually was a little embarrassing, but the Pastor told us one night, "Don't worry about it because there will come a time where you won't have any problems finding the books in the bible." We laughed a "yeah, right" laugh, but we kept coming. Before long, we were able to find the scriptures without having to go to the index.

I still had some issues, but I was striving to make life better for us. Little by little my life began to change. I began to pray and ask God to change me, change my life, and change my habits. I wanted to live a life of holiness but it would be a long road to getting there.

Since I had made up my mind to live for Christ, things in my life began to happen. I didn't know that attacks from the enemy (demonic spirits) were sure to come, that they would be included in the process.

I was driving a silver Sable, and it was nice! I hadn't had it for more than a year, when sitting in my driveway it caught fire in the middle of the night. The insurance had lapsed the week prior, and I was just waiting on payday to get it renewed. I still had three years to pay for a car that I did not have. This was my first lesson in spiritual warfare and humility.

It took everything in me to continue to go to church. I just wanted to quit church, life and my job. I thought everything was supposed to get easier once you began to live for Christ. I didn't know that I would encounter spiritual warfare.

What I also didn't know was that God was working on me in the process. Instead of driving to work in a nice car, I was reduced to catching the bus and getting rides to church from people who didn't really want to pick me up. I understood why; I'm sure it had to be an inconvenience. I was grateful, especially since I didn't even have the finances to pay them.

This was an on-and-off time of fellowship for me. It took everything out of me to ask people to do anything for me. I got a couple of cars during this process, but they always broke down quickly. I didn't have the money to purchase a car that would run for more than a couple of months. Yet, I pressed on.

During this time, many things had changed in my life. Nekita and Terry had moved to the east side. Jay had begun seeing a woman with a child, and he was in and out of the house, so it was just Tiffany and myself.

My friend Wilda and her family had joined church. We both had begun to get our lives in order. When I was able to get a car, I decided to get a van, something that I could transport people back and forth to church in.

I didn't want anyone to have to go through what I'd had to endure. It had been a long three years, and I was looking forward to my independence or freedom to be able to come and go as I pleased.

Other things had changed as well. My drinking and partying had just about been eliminated completely. I didn't like the way drinking made me feel, so my desire for it had changed. I hated the smell and taste of alcohol. But I often laugh because my drink of choice had been Christian Brothers Brandy—thinking that, even in my drunken state, God had his hand on me.

It was time for the next chapter in my life to begin...

10. Taking the Next Step

There was one part of my life that I needed to get under control. I loved the Lord and desired to live for him, and I had been praying that my friend Cornell would give his life to Christ, totally. Helen Baylor used to sing a song called "Can You Help My Friend?", and I would sing this song, praying and seeking God for Cornell to turn his life around. Some of his secrets had been exposed, and I was trying to deal with them. However, I would not let them hinder my walk with Christ. I was determined to get this thing right. All of my life, I had had to struggle, and most of the time I'd failed. I didn't want that to happen again.

My first step was to locate my husband and let him know that I wanted a divorce. He agreed and asked me if I was getting married. At that time, I had no definite plans to get married, but I needed to get my life in order. As we sat talking as old friends, I was able to witness to him and lead him to Christ. I ushered the very person who'd caused so much pain in my life into a relationship with Christ.

Why couldn't I treat people the way they treated me? Why couldn't I abuse their emotions the way they abused me? I couldn't. I never have been able to hold grudges. I only want the best for others; I've always been like that, even as a child.

Cornell and I would spend every Friday night together. It usually consisted of dinner, television or a movie, and sexual dessert. It had gotten to the point that, after we left each other on Saturday morning, I would have to deal with the guilt of being in sin.

By this time Cornell had come to church with me and accepted Jesus Christ as his Lord and Savior, but decided to join another church where his parents and most of his family attended. We were now both serving God but with two different visions. His church was a traditional church, where pretty much everything was accepted, and my church was teaching and preaching holiness.

Needless to say, we struggled with our walk together. I had gotten to the point where I couldn't do it anymore; either we were going to get married and get out of fornication, or the relationship would have to end. Remember, I wasn't looking for a relationship! But I could no longer live in sin.

We both knew that something had to change, so we decided to get married. We got engaged but didn't talk about a wedding. We were engaged but never made plans for or discussed our future. Fortunately, or unfortunately, we realized that neither one of us was ready for such a commitment. So I gave him back the ring.

Over the course of the next year or so, we continued to see each other, but it was different. I would go home on Friday nights instead of spending the night; we were spending less time with each other and more time in our respective churches. He had begun to be trained as a Deacon, and I was soaking up as much of the Word of God as I could handle.

I also had begun focusing more on my daughter Tiffany, and my nieces and nephews. They were all part of one of the only black swim teams in the Detroit area, and I was the driver for most of the family. This allowed me to stop focusing so much on Cornell and more on my personal life.

I remember that, when I was finally able to discuss our future with Cornell, we both realized (at the same time) that this was a "do-or-die" situation.

Either we were going to go all the way (get married), or we were walking away from this relationship. At this point, we had been seeing each other for almost ten years. We had time invested into this relationship. Did we just want to throw it all away? If it meant me living a life pleasing to God or staying in sin, I was willing to let it all go, and so was he.

In January of 1998, I had transferred from VA Medical Center to become a City Carrier at the US Postal Service, and I was determined to move forward in life. A new job and a new life (with or without Cornell). Then, in March of 1998, while having dinner at a Coney Island restaurant, he proposed again (this time with the help of my daughter Tiffany).

Our wedding was planned, and in August 1998, I became Mrs. Cornell Fox. I had no idea what lay ahead of me.

Even before the wedding, I realized that I wasn't the only one with deep hidden secrets. Just as I did, my husband had many, many secrets.

I had often wondered why I only met some of his family; one of his nieces wanted to know as well. She was pretending as if she wanted to be in the wedding just to inquire about our relationship. "Well, why hasn't he brought you around the family? Well, if you have been dating this long, how come we never heard about you?" Funny how things happen; *I* was a well-kept secret. I had been outmatched by the best.

Some of the things that happened before and after the wedding shook the very core of our relationship. However, because I was a woman of faith, I would not allow others to see or even perceive that our marriage was a "mistake," so I pressed on through some very difficult times.

I had to deal with the ex-wife from hell (I will just say it—not to offend anyone, just to state the truth). However, I don't blame her. I think to a certain extent we were both victims of lies and betrayal. Unfortunately, neither of us has ever had an opportunity to try and at least be civil to one another. But that would not be.

As a result, I was never afforded a real opportunity to develop a relationship with Cornell's children from his previous marriage—or with most of his family, in all honesty. However, I do thank God for his mom and dad and his sisters. They never treated me any other way but nice, and for that, I am profoundly grateful. But I don't fit in, and I'm okay with that. (Remember, in my first book, *The*

Forgotten Child, I explained that I was used to "not fitting in." It is something I have come to expect.)

It's easy to function when you know your place, so I stay there. I snicker when I see them struggling with whether they can even mention his ex-wife's name in my presence. As if I didn't know he had a wife before me, it would be funny if it wasn't so sad. So I retreat within myself as my safety mechanism, and I find it very disappointing.

Cornell has always been and continues to be such a BIG part of my family's lives. My daughter calls and treats him as Dad, my son acknowledges him as Mr. Fox (in a reverential kind of way) or Pops. My grandchildren refer to him as Grandad. I would never want to take his ex-wife's place, but it would be nice to be able to love them just as I love my own.

As I write this book, we have been together 30 years and married for over 20 years, and it still has not been ratified and I have come to accept the fact that it never will be.

What's even sadder is that his ex-wife never got over it. I don't know what lies behind the secrets, but it has affected others deeply. I have so much love to give. I can just add this to another one of those "broken-heart" experiences.

As we became one, I was instructed to join my husband at his church, which was a culture shock to me. Nonetheless, I pressed on and tried to find my position. It was at "this church" that I watched my husband (as a Deacon in training) baptize his ex-wife. Yes, she actually joined the church that we were going to. His entire family went to that church, so it was no surprise that she would join. I thought it was a little strange that you would subject yourself to that situation, especially when you had no desire to try to develop some type of relationship with his current wife.

However, I was mature enough to handle it, but it cut like a knife. Wounds that run deep, wounds that still affect our marriage, unknowingly. See, I have learned to live with this secret. I have learned to ignore it, to walk away. But, make no mistake about it, it has had an impact. I choose not to deal with the craziness. I choose not to deal with the "secrets." However, I have and I do hold my husband personally responsible for the state that this relationship is in. The secrets he held have gotten us to this place, and now I am done with this part of our lives. Whatever went on between him and his ex-wife is between them; I have moved on, and I choose not to allow it to interrupt my happiness.

When I first started attending the church services with my husband, I noticed things that I warned my husband about. Unfortunately, all the warnings fell on deaf ears, would eventually come to light. It wasn't long before the church would split.

The one thing that we both had in common was loyalty to leadership, and we decided to go with the Pastor. I was always taught to respect leadership and we both felt that it was the right thing to do. Within a couple of years, we found ourselves at odds with the church, and we eventually stepped away from it church completely. I won't go into much detail because I believe that is between them and God.

Out of fellowship—but not out of Love with God—I (we) had had enough of the church thing! We loved God, respected God; we just didn't want a relationship with the people of God.

My home church was having difficulties too, and I felt that most of the congregation was just hypocrites. As I look back, I realize that this feeling was mostly the result of the pain that we had experienced, but my mind was made up: "My Mother would be My Ministry." No matter how bad it got, I never lost faith in God.

11. Saving My Mother's Honor

By this time, my mother started attending church with us; she had become an usher and was excited. It was good to worship with Mama again. My mother had also been diagnosed with dementia, and I began to care for her. I am so grateful that we were able to allow her to experience some of the good things in life while she was able to enjoy them.

One of the things that we discovered was our love for traveling. I had always heard that my in-laws traveled a lot, and I was grateful when we were able to join them. We became travel buddies, and my mom was included, and they welcomed her with open arms. We were able to take her to several of my husband's family's reunions as well as on a trip to Hawaii. It meant so much to me to see her so happy.

The reality of her disease set in when we were on our flight to Honolulu and she would not get out of the seat for nine hours. (I realize now she was afraid). She also would tell me to look at the angel on the wing (it was actually her reflection in the mirror, but she didn't realize it). She was so happy, and that made me happy.

(I would just like to say that I am forever indebted to my mother- and father-in-love as well as my sister-in-love Leana Fox. Thank you for making my mom your priority, too.)

It was during one of these trips that we really noticed my mom's declining mental capacity. She had left of her hotel room and got lost. One of Cornell's nieces brought her back to us. When we returned home, her employer also called me and told me that they had been noticing her mental decline and urged me to take her in to see Dr. Terry Scott Baul.

My mother had helped Dr. Baul as an intern, and now he would be responsible for taking care of her. He was known all over the east side of Detroit, and I was confident that, if anything was going on with her, he would let us know. So, we set up the doctor's appointment to hear the diagnosis that we already knew was coming. This was something we couldn't wish away; we couldn't pretend it didn't exist. We needed to get her some help. Of course, Mama was in denial (as we had been) and reassured us that there was nothing wrong with her.

She was living with my sister and her children, but it seemed to be overwhelming for her. I spoke with my siblings, and we agreed that we would move Mama into a Senior Citizen Apartment. I thought that a slower pace of life would help her to focus a little easier. Also, it was time for Mama to retire. I know this had to be difficult for her because she had worked all of her life. She seemed so lost. Waking up with nowhere to go, with someone planning her day and deciding what she would eat or wear. It was so heartbreaking to witness, yet it had to be done.

Knowing that she would not be able to stay there alone, I decided I would stay with her during the week and my sister or niece would care for her on the weekends. Since my husband and I were going through changes regarding the "secrets" and the issues with his ex-wife, I felt, in my mind, that this was my way of leaving him. I didn't have to deal with that issue, and I could keep the secret of things not working out as I thought they should have.

The arrangement was that my brother would be with her during the day while I was at work and I would go back to her apartment to prepare dinner and spend the night.

I actually enjoyed being with her, and we had some good times listening to gospel music and dancing around the apartment.

It was during this time that my grandfather passed away, and it was customary that the oldest child would handle all of the affairs. As we lay in bed one night, my mother informed me that she did not want her siblings to know she was sick (I am not so sure that she had fully accepted it), so she asked me to look over her shoulder to make sure everything was done correctly. We pulled it off. No one knew she was ill, and I felt that she was grateful that I was there.

Once the funeral was over it was time to settle my grandfather's estate. Since My grandfather had a lot of property and insurance policies with no living beneficiaries, we were headed to Probate Court.

After securing a lawyer, my mother and her siblings set up a bank account. Every one of my grandfather's assets would have to be deposited into this account. When it was all collected, the siblings would sell the property and divide the assets among themselves. But then there were problems.

One of my cousins had gotten my grandfather to sign over all of his property to him. The children were furious! My mother, my Aunt Joan, and my Uncle Doug would meet regularly to try and find out what could be done. It wasn't so much about the property as it was about the betrayal. They felt betrayed by someone who had no legal right to the property.

My Uncle Doug was so upset he had a heart attack. The night before he passed away, I took Mama to the hospital to see him, and the last thing he said to me was "I hope I live long enough to see your cousin pay for what he has done." Uncle Doug passed away the next morning. We were heartbroken and devastated.

This was Mama's closest brother and the last one living. My mother experienced two deaths within a period of two or three months. The experiences caused her so much pain, and, no matter how I tried to cheer her up or make her forget about it, I could see the sadness in her eyes. Her spirit had been crushed.

Once my uncle died, it seemed as if the Probate case slowed up. The money from the various life-insurance policies had been deposited into the bank, and we were just waiting for the court to see how the finances would be distributed.

Around this time, I had gotten wind that my niece was having my mom co-sign a loan or something for her. I didn't like it and I told my mom it wasn't a good idea. I should add that this was a niece that my mom raised from birth, so she was very, very close to her.

I thought it was a dead subject until one morning I was preparing to go to work and my niece showed up. *This early in the morning? What's going on?* Needless to say, I was running late and had to go. When I tried to discuss this with my mother, it became a place of contention so I would limit the conversations. She would become so angry, not wanting anyone to tell her what to do. Still trying to hold onto the little independence she had left.

As already mentioned, the arrangement was that I would stay with my mom after work, my brother would stay with her during the day, my sister would assist my brother, and my niece would help on the weekends. I noticed that my niece and sister were spending more time with my mom during the week, but, when it came time for me to go home on the weekends, they wouldn't be there. As a result, my mom would be with my husband and me more and more on the weekends or I would stay at her apartment with her, listening to gospel music and dancing around the apartment.

My mother worked in the neighborhood pharmacy and everyone knew her. However, she always felt that she needed money on her and would become very agitated when we tried to take it away. It was during this time that she began to walk out of the house more frequently. She would try to leave the apartment, but Li'l Bro would lie across the doorway so she could not get out. Unfortunately, at our house she had full access and would get out quickly. I knew her safety was becoming an issue.

After attending a church service, a new house was spoken into my life. My husband and I had discussed moving before, but with no urgency. Now it seemed like a necessity instead of a desire. I had spoken to Li'l Bro and informed him that we would be willing to take Mama with us. He agreed, and the house search began.

Everything was fine until we got ready to move. I received a lot of push back from Mama about the location: it was too far from the city.

So I agreed to keep her apartment in the city so that, when my Li'l Bro and Ellen would have my mom, they would have a place for her to rest. There was one condition: they would have to pay the rent.

I knew it would only be a matter of time before the rent wouldn't be paid and we would have to move Mama out, but, to appease them, I agreed to the arrangement. See, the support had already started to fade away, and her care was being left up to my husband and me—and Tiffany. She was always willing to help.

I spoke with the representative of the apartment complex and explained the situation. I asked her to please let me know if the rent got behind and I would ensure that it was paid. It didn't take long before I received a call saying that my mother was being evicted from her apartment. I made arrangements to come and make the past-due payments. At this time, I also spoke with my family and told them that the only thing I wanted from the apartment was my mother's bedroom set so that she would have a bed in her room at our new house.

Moving day came, and, when I got to the apartment with my mother, all of her things had already been divided. It was as if my mother was already dead. The only thing that hadn't been taken or assigned out was her clothing. I was so upset. I put my mother back in the car and drove towards home, crying. I called my husband, and he calmed me down, told me to go get my mother a bedroom set on the way home, and then come home. The hurt of that day still lingers. I had made up in my mind that day that I was done with my family. From then on, it was all about taking care of my mother.

During the house-buying process, I was promoted to a supervisor position at the United States Postal Service and would have to travel to Oklahoma for a total of twelve weeks. Three weeks away and three weeks home. During this time, my husband shared the responsibility of caring for my mother with my family. My daughter was completing her first year of college and everything was changing.

When things settled down and I settled into my new job, I was now working midnights. This allowed me to be with my mother during the day, and my husband would care for her at night.

Also, I was able to get back to setting my mother's personal business in order.

It was during one of these times that I discovered that her personal bank account had been wiped out. As we sat in front of the bank representative, it became obvious that someone had forged her signature. Over $10,000 had been depleted from her account.

Fortunately, all the money was replaced. However, it never dawned on me to look at the checking account that was in Probate Court. I wasn't aware of anyone even knowing about that account. What I didn't take into consideration was that my mother's bank statements were being delivered to her old address, even though I had put in a change of address with the Post Office.

What I soon discovered was that this bank account had also been wiped out. This made me so sick I vomited. To think that someone would treat my mother this way broke my heart into a million pieces. Someone had taken all of my mom's sibling money to the tune of over $40,000. How in the world could someone do this to someone that they said they loved? This left me not just broken but shattered.

I immediately went to the bank to file a complaint and then contacted the lawyer's office.

I was in a panic and in total disbelief. *What am I supposed to do?* I had to save my mother's honor. How could I tell her family that the very thing that they were so heartbroken about when it came to my cousin and grandfather had happened in my family, due to my mother's loved ones? The very ones that she sacrificed her life for. The very ones that she protected, time and time again. The very ones that meant so much to her. How could they do this, *Lord, help me!*

I had to file a lawsuit against the bank to try to retrieve these finances. The bank said its only obligation was to make sure that the person whose name was on the account was present. It didn't matter about the person's mental capacity, that wasn't the bank's problem. As long as my mother was present, with ID, the funds were legally hers.

However, the evidence was clear. Someone had taken my mother into the bank and through the drive-through, withdrawing money. Sometimes more than once a day.

Unfortunately, my mother had no idea what was going on. She was just happy to be riding. In the mental state that she was in, she just wanted to go for a ride. As long as she was riding and eating shrimp, she was satisfied. And they played on it.

Not only did they make numerous trips to the bank, but one of my relatives actually wrote herself a $10,000 check. I'm still amazed that they could not be prosecuted legally for elder abuse. If I would have had the opportunity to prosecute, I definitely would have!

You don't treat people this way. Yes, I have forgiven, but it has put many things in perspective for me.

I am like my mother in so many different ways, but I promised myself this is one thing. I would not follow in her footsteps when it came to caring for my grandchildren. My mother always protected my sister and gave up her life to care for the children of others. I saw how they repaid her, by stealing money that didn't belong to them, not bothering to visit and generally showing a lack of concern. When she had nothing else to give, they were gone (under the pretense of "not wanting to see her like this")—it still breaks my heart every time I think about it.

I applaud those families that are able to come together and share in the care of their elders; I applaud those families that can come together in unity; I applaud those families that don't fall apart when our elders go home to be with the Lord. Unfortunately, my family just didn't happen to be one of them.

Looking back, I remember one Saturday when my mom and I were driving up to visit my daughter at college and one of my nephews called me to see where his mother (Ellen) was. She had promised him that she was going to take him to the bank. It didn't dawn on me that they would actually steal from my mother and that they would be all right with that. Jesus, what kind of family is this?

The Forgotten Child resurfaced, and I walked away from the entire family. Family doesn't treat you like this. Family doesn't use and abuse you. I've learned to forgive. I've learned to let things go. I've learned to move forward. Understanding that true healing starts from the inside out. But, who does this? I felt like they were monsters!

I could not tell anyone what was happening. I did not want anyone to know that my mother's children and grandchildren had robbed her and her sibling's blind. Sadly, my Aunt Joan passed away without knowing the truth about what happened. But I had to save my mother's honor.

This separation went on for years. My husband and I were busy taking care of mama, and I left my family to do whatever they did. My brother would come by from time to time to see Mama, but she had very few visitors. Outside of my Aunt Marlene, who would come and stay with us to help care for mom, it was just us. Mama did have a wonderful respite caregiver, Evenly Crispell, who came out a couple times a week to give us a break. She would bathe and minister to mama through song and the Word of God.

In January or February of 2010, I began receiving text messages that invited me to "come and worship with us at church." I actually didn't know who was sending the texts, which continued to come every week. Once I found out who it was, I quickly decided that this was something that I didn't want to be a part of.

There was no way I was going to that church. First of all, I didn't want anything to do with my family. And secondly, I didn't want to get caught up in that "church thing" again. I had dealt with enough pain from church people; they would not be able to hurt me again. So, for months, I said "no."

Before long, everyone was texting me asking me to come to church. My brother, my daughter and other family members were now part of this church.

So I reluctantly decided to go and check it out. When I got there, I could see what all the fuss was about. The Pastor reminded me so much of my Beloved Pastor Leon Glover—even the environment seemed right. Before long, I was dropping in to visit. While visiting, I found out that the church was in the process of moving. I decided I would attend church until they moved, but once they moved, I was done.

However, God had other plans.

After the move, I still would drop in (after work) and would hurriedly leave after service. I didn't want a relationship with these people, only with the Word. Eventually, that would change as well. The more I came, the more I wanted to be there. I missed the fellowship, I missed praise and worship, and I missed being in the presence of God. In April 2010, I finally joined and became a part of this church.

I had decided to give my mom a 78th birthday party in April of that year, and I invited the Pastor and First Lady to come and celebrate with us. This allowed them to come and meet my husband because he was still wounded and offended from the last church that we belonged to.

At the time, I didn't really understand that this church that I joined would carry me for the next couple of years through much grief and pain. This was a healing place for me, where I would be given the opportunity to forgive my family for the things that they had done to my mother. *It wasn't about me, but you came against my mother. It hurt me that you would do something so cruel to my mother.* I knew I needed to forgive—not for them but for myself.

What I didn't know is that the course of my life was about to change. In August of 2010, my husband and I had planned an anniversary trip. It had been years since we had been away together because someone always had to be here to care for mama. The day before we were supposed to depart, my mother was admitted into Harper Hospital.

Due to an accident with a reclining lift chair my mother, had become bed ridden. Not only was she bed ridden but she also had been on a feeding tube for years. My husband would usually drive my mother to the hospital because she had become bed ridden, and I was unable to get her out of the car.

I had worked the night before, and I remember that I was exhausted. So exhausted, that I went out to sleep in the car because I couldn't take it any longer. As usual, I called everyone to let them know Mama had been admitted, Not that I expected anyone to come see her, but I still felt that they had a right to know. When they found out that we had been planning to go on vacation, they urged us to still go, and they promised that they would be there to take care of Mama.

The day we arrived back home was the same day she was discharged from the hospital. Only this time when she came home, she was different. She had come home with oxygen assistance and bedsores. During her many years of being bedridden, she had never had a bed sore. This told me that no one had been there with her to ask for her to be turned over, or asked for her to be changed. They promised to be there, and again they lied. What I did learn is that I can't expect everyone to operate in the same manner that I did. Everyone didn't have that level of commitment. This was the beginning of the end.

On October 29 (my birthday), Mama was admitted again to the hospital. The bedsores had become infected, and she would need a central line in order for them to give her IV antibiotics. When they took her down to surgery, she aspirated on the table, and some fluid got into her lungs. They didn't know if she would make it through the night and told us to call our family to come to the hospital. I watched as they came, one by one. I stood back and watched, and it all seemed unreal to me. They filed in like they loved her so much but my only thought was where you have been? You come now when it appears that she's about to die but you couldn't come say hello, or call to check on her.

I totally blocked their presence out of my mind. I can remember just saying, "Mama, please don't leave me on my birthday. Mama, please!"

She made it through the night and the next night and the next night. She was far from out of the woods, but she was still here. She stayed in Harper Hospital until around Thanksgiving, when they transferred her to another hospital. This one seemed to be the place for patients who were too sick for a Nursing Home but required long-term care.

After she was transferred, Pastor Sherome Ivory came to visit me. I don't know why I began to share with him all that I had gone through with my family, but, before I realized it, I had shared everything regarding the bank accounts, why I wasn't close to my family, and what I believed God was saying to me about reuniting with my family. People's Church of Holiness would be the place that God would use to bring us back together. It felt good to release all of the hurt, pain, and shame!

The last two months of her life, my schedule consisted of coming home every two days for a shower and to get clean clothes, then go back to the hospital. The doctors have given me several options for placing my mom in another hospital, and I opted for the one that would be closest to her family. I was certain that, if she was right there in the neighborhood, I would get some help. Unfortunately, that would not be a reality.

My mother's favorite part of the year was Christmas. When I was a child, we would go Christmas shopping for hours. She just liked to look. It was no wonder that God would take her home on Dec 27th. Two days prior to that on Christmas Day, I was so tired I laid my head on the side of the bed and cried, partly because I was tired and because no one even bothered to come see her (Ellen came and stayed five minutes). Everyone else had their own lives to live, that didn't include Mama.

I don't care how you try to prepare for it, when you lose someone so close; it cuts you to your very core. There is no escaping it, and there is no preparation for it. It just happens, it just is!

When my mom went home to be with the Lord, my world was turned upside down. I had lost myself in the process of caring for my mom. I didn't understand it then when her nurses would encourage me to take some time for myself. It was only after her passing that I realized that self-care is just as important as caring for those you love.

During the course of my grief experience I came to understand that grief actually saved my life. All my life, I ran from many things. I ran from the pain of childhood to the pain of abuse—the pain of disappointment and guilt and shame. However, during my grief process I had to acknowledge that I had no control over anything and my true healing would have to come from God. As Iyanla Vanzant says, "I had to do the work," and it was and continues to be a painful but necessary process.

Healing would have to begin from the "Inside out."

Beautifully Broken: To My Readers

This book has been written to every man or woman who has ever had to deal with any type of physical or emotional abuse. Abuse can cause you to lose focus of your self-worth and even your personal identity. When you're faced with many of life's challenges, it can become easier to retreat within by not dealing with the pain, frustration, or disappointments that life can bring. Also, emotional and physical abuse not only causes havoc to *your* personal lives but affects those around you.

Physical and emotional abuse can be used as a catalyst to push us into a place of just going through the motions of life. Not really living but existing. For far too many of us, it has become easier to just give in, losing ourselves in the process. Fear becomes a normal part of our lives, and we believe that's what life entails for us. Nothing could be further from the truth!

It can be especially difficult to witness those that we love being abused. Especially when we are living in a day and time where elder abuse is not something that we've heard about—but it's happening in almost every family (in one form or another).

In this book, I talk about elder abuse and how it's usually at the hand of someone that the elder loves and trusts. If other family members witness this abuse, it can tear the family asunder, and only God will be able to reunite the family. I acknowledge this abuse because it is real, and it is devastating to everyone involved.

In order for healing to take place, we must first acknowledge that we are *broken*. Admit that things are not always what they seem. Most of us have become masters of deception. We shield and protect our "secrets" that lead us to heartbreak and loneliness—mostly because of our pride and because we don't want others to know just how vulnerable we are. However, it's only when we admit that we are wounded that we can begin the healing process. Whether it is caused by unforgiveness, resentment, pride, or other issues, we must identify our problem and desire to be free from the pain of our past. It is only when we begin to visit those secret places of hurt and shame that we can truly discover how powerful we really are.

Beautifully Broken

Beautifully Broken describes how I once was lost but, through the grace of God, was found. This book has been written for you to know that you are not alone. I've made many mistakes and bad decisions in my life, but God has a way of turning it all around so that it will work out for my good. So that we can be "Healed from the Inside Out."

"For we know that in all things God works for the good of those who love him, who have been called according to his purpose." Romans 8:28

Pastor Dr. Donna Fox

Beautifully Broken: I Say a Little Prayer for You

Father God, I come before You today, first giving You praise and glory for Your loving kindness towards Your children.

Father, I ask, if there be anything in us that is not of You, that You would remove it now in Jesus' Name.

Lord, we come asking You to help us to forgive others that may have used or abused us during our life. Help us to forgive ourselves for making decisions that were contrary to Your will for our lives.

Give us a desire for a clean heart and renew a right spirit within us.

Give us a desire to overcome all the adversities that have come to weigh us down.

We want to be made whole.

We want to be made new in You.

Beautifully Broken

We Thank You for a New Beginning with a new look on life and Another Chance to Start (ACTS)

Help us to know that we have been fearfully and wonderfully made.

Thank You for restoring us back unto Yourself.

In Jesus' Name,

Amen

www.ingramcontent.com/pod-product-compliance
Lightning Source LLC
Chambersburg PA
CBHW031151160426
43193CB00008B/325